the five dilemmas of Calvinism

CRAIG R. BROWN

LIGONIER MINISTRIES
ORLANDO FLORIDA

The Five Dilemmas of Calvinism
© 2007 by Craig R. Brown

Published by Ligonier Ministries
400 Technology Park, Lake Mary, FL 32746

Printed in the United States of America

Cover design: Geoff Stevens
Interior design and typeset: Katherine Lloyd, Sisters, Oregon

Library of Congress Cataloging-in-Publication Data
Brown, Craig R., 1956-
 The five dilemmas of Calvinism / by Craig R. Brown.
     p. cm.
 ISBN 1-56769-086-6
1. Calvinism. 2. Reformed Church–Doctrines. 3. Theology, Doctrinal.
I. Title.
 BX9422.3.B76 2007
 230'.42–dc22

                                        2007016234

table of contents

foreword

Any system of doctrine that attempts in the slightest degree to be faithful to Scripture will be difficult to understand. The things of God are deep, challenging matters that require concerted mental labor to master. It is true that the essentials of the gospel are within reach of those who are very young, but as the author of Hebrews points out, "everyone who lives on milk is unskilled in the word of righteousness, since he is a child. But solid food is for the mature, for those who have their powers of discernment trained by constant practice" (Heb. 5:13–14a). In other words, there is much to the Scriptures and the Christian faith beyond what immediately meets the eye, and it is not easy to get at it—"constant practice" is necessary to move from the "unskilled" state to that of "mature" and "trained." Even Peter acknowledged the difficulty of doctrine when he said of the letters of his colleague Paul, the apostle who, more than any other, laid down the doctrinal basics of the Christian faith: "There are some things in them that are hard to understand" (2 Peter 3:16b). He was right. For this reason, I would be suspicious of any doctrinal system I could thoroughly grasp with ease.

Calvinism is certainly no easy system to master. But in addition to being difficult to understand, Calvinism is often the subject of grave *misunderstanding*, simply because it is so counterintuitive and countercultural. As George Whitefield, the evangelist of the Great Awakening, once declared, "We are all Arminians by nature." Simply put, the tenets of Arminianism taste sweeter to our sinful human natures than those of other doctrinal systems. Not surprisingly, these teachings are affirmed and ingrained in us by the culture and, sadly, by immense segments of the church. Thus, it ought not surprise us that, upon hearing the doctrines of grace for the first time, Arminian Christians often are quick to jump to inaccurate conclusions about the tenets of this system that Calvinists believe most accurately summarizes the teachings of Scripture.

It is at precisely this point that this book you are holding proves its worth to the church—both the Calvinist and Arminian branches. In these pages, Craig Brown battles misunderstandings that have dogged Calvinism for long years. In so doing, he provides apologetic help for Calvinists stymied by the misinformed questions of their Arminian friends. And, of course, he kindles light for those who have never considered alternatives to the Arminian system.

Scripture-saturated, winsome, honest—this book is all of these and more. May it be used greatly by the Spirit of God to bring understanding by dispelling misunderstanding.

—R. C. SPROUL
Orlando, Florida
January 2007

Introduction

The overriding purpose of this book is to defend the Reformed faith, sometimes known as Calvinism, against some of the misconceptions that have hindered its acceptance by the modern Christian community. As with all misconceptions, there exists a fundamental lack of knowledge concerning the truth about Calvinism. I hope this book can help fill that knowledge gap.

In my defense of the Reformed faith, I will be "the Devil's advocate" and attack five principles of Calvinism from the standpoint of American "common sense." I will ask—and answer—the logical questions that arise in the minds of every student of theology and every Christian as they are confronted with Reformed theology for the first time. I want to show that not only does Calvinism have answers to the five dilemmas I will put forward, it has the only answers that fit with Scripture.

It is my hope that this book will:

1. Comfort those of us who hold to Reformed doctrine but who continually question it because of perceived inconsistencies in it.
2. Challenge those Christians who adhere to Arminian doctrine to look at the Reformed faith with an open mind and attempt to see the consistency of this system and the honor it gives to God.
3. Eliminate the argument of unbelievers that Christianity is a religion of distortions, contradictions, and ritual, and to display the beauty of a totally loving God who has called His people to Himself from the foundation of the world.

I have designed this book be a simple, easy read for the person who has questions and is struggling to find the answers. Chapters 1 and 2 set the historical and doctrinal foundation for Calvinism. Chapters 3–7 discuss five major dilemmas that confront every Christian who considers the Reformed faith. A suggested list for more detailed reading can be found after the conclusion.

The following passages from the Scriptures give us a foundation for understanding the mysteries of God's sovereignty. I encourage you to meditate on them as you prayerfully consider the information you are about to read.

"God thunders wondrously with his voice; he does great things that we cannot comprehend." (Job 37:5)

Great is our Lord, and abundant in power; his understanding is beyond measure. (Ps. 147:5)

"I am God, and there is no other; I am God, and there is none like me, declaring the end from the beginning and from ancient times things not yet done, saying, 'My counsel shall stand, and I will accomplish all my purpose.'" (Isa. 46:9b–10)

"For my thoughts are not your thoughts, neither are your ways my ways, declares the Lord. For as the heavens are higher than the earth, so are my ways higher than your ways and my thoughts than your thoughts." (Isa. 55:8–9)

"Call to me and I will answer you, and will tell you great and hidden things that you have not known." (Jer. 33:3)

"With God all things are possible." (Matt. 19:26b)

"It is not for you to know times or seasons that the Father has fixed by his own authority." (Acts 1:7b)

Oh, the depth of the riches and wisdom and knowledge of God! How unsearchable are his judgments and how inscrutable his ways! "For who has known the mind of the

Lord, or who has been his counselor?" "Or who has given a gift to him that he might be repaid?" For from him and through him and to him are all things. To him be glory forever! (Rom. 11:33–36)

We impart a secret and hidden wisdom of God, which God decreed before the ages for our glory. (1 Cor. 2:7)

It is my hope and prayer that, after reading this book, you will have a truer understanding of the belief system known as Calvinism and a new appreciation for historical Christianity and the truth that can set your mind free. I thank all who take the time to read this book, meditate on its truths, and pray about its conclusions.

—Craig Brown
Charlottesville, Virginia
January 2007

Chapter 1

True and False Teaching

What is the historical basis for Reformed theology (Calvinism)?

When you hear the word *doctrine*, what do you think of first? For many, the words *boring* and *unimportant* come to mind. But doctrine is just a way of stating an understanding of what the Bible teaches. In other words, a doctrine is a teaching.

All Christians have doctrines that help to explain what they believe. Reformed Christians are no exception. The doctrines held by Reformed Christians are similar to those of other Christians in some ways and distinctive in others. However, I want to show in these first two chapters that the

Reformed faith is closer to the teachings of Jesus and Paul in the Scriptures than any other form of the Christian religion.

Let me begin with a quick review of church history.

The Bible tells us that the church will always face heresies and needs to be prepared to deal with them. The apostle Peter wrote, "But false prophets also arose among the people, just as there will be false teachers among you, who will secretly bring in destructive heresies, even denying the Master who bought them, bringing upon themselves swift destruction" (2 Peter 2:1).

Unorthodox teachings were not unusual in the first five hundred years after the time of Christ. When such teachings arose, the church recognized its responsibility to investigate them, determine their validity, and state the truth in a clear manner. To accomplish this goal, church councils were called to discuss important subjects. These councils included:

- The Council of Nicaea (AD 325), which proclaimed that Christ is God (the Nicene Creed is recited in many churches).
- The Council of Constantinople (381), which proclaimed that the Holy Spirit is God.
- The Council of Ephesus (431), which proclaimed that human beings are totally depraved from birth.

- The Council of Chalcedon (451), which proclaimed that Christ is both God and man.

The Council of Ephesus was called in response to a prominent false teaching known as Pelagianism, named after its founder, Pelagius, a British monk. He denied that the human race fell into original sin with Adam. Babies, he said, are not born corrupt but innocent. They become bad when they grow up, through the bad examples of others. It is their environment that makes them bad, not original sin.

Pelagius was opposed by Augustine, the bishop of Hippo in North Africa. Augustine was the greatest theologian of the early church. He spent much of his life defending the orthodox or true faith against heresies. Fighting these battles helped him codify the doctrines that were taught by Jesus and Paul in the Scriptures.

In his response to Pelagius, Augustine taught that every man is conceived and born in sin, and can be saved only through the grace of God according to His good pleasure. The Council of Ephesus eventually agreed, declaring the teachings of Pelagius to be heresy.

About one hundred years later, Cassian developed what is known as Semi-Pelagianism. This doctrinal system taught that man is able to take the first steps toward conversion with his own powers. According to Semi-Pelagianism, God's grace is available to all men, but the final decision in each individual case is dependent on the exercise of free will. In 529, the Synod of Orange condemned the teaching of Semi-Pelagianism as heresy.

However, despite these positive stands for orthodoxy, the church quickly fell into a state of corruption and impurity. The church was persecuted by the Roman Empire in varying degrees for its first three hundred years, depending upon the will of the emperors, all of whom were heathen. Then, in 313, Emperor Constantine, who had become a professing Christian, issued the Edict of Milan, which made Christianity legal. Soon it became the state religion of the empire. While this edict had the positive effect of eliminating persecution, it had a negative impact on the purity of the church. Suddenly, everyone wanted to become a Christian to assure himself a position in the Roman establishment. The moniker of *Christian* became a passport to political, military, and social promotion. Thousands of heathens joined the church and corruption quickly followed.

When Rome fell to the Goths in 410, civilization was set back. For the next thousand years, known as the "Middle Ages," the church became entwined in the affairs of the state; in essence, the two entities became one. The low quality of church leadership, the abuse of power, and the temptation of wealth all contributed to a great decline in the purity of the church.

This was the atmosphere when Martin Luther arrived on the scene in the early sixteenth century. Disturbed by the condition of the church, Luther, a German monk, invited debate by posting his Ninety-Five Theses on the castle church door in Wittenberg. His goal was to reform the church and return it to the purity of its early years. Instead, he became the first of a number of Reformers who eventually led a movement away from the Roman Catholic Church, a movement that we know today as Protestantism. This was not a new religion but a return to the truth, the teachings, the *doctrine*, of the early church.

Luther was the main Reformer in Germany, and his followers were called Lutherans. John Calvin was the main Reformer in France and Switzerland, and his followers were called Reformed believers. John Knox was the Reformer in Scotland, and his followers were called Presbyterians.

Each church developed its own confession of faith, but they all agreed on the basic doctrines of Scripture and stressed the biblical teachings of Paul as they had been interpreted by Augustine and the early church leaders. In his book, *Institutes of the Christian Religion*, Calvin put down on paper the doctrines that were the foundation for all

Protestant groups at the time of the Reformation—especially the sovereignty of God in salvation.

In his "Historical and Theological Introduction" to Luther's *The Bondage of the Will,* J. I. Packer writes:

> All the leading Protestant theologians of the first epoch of the Reformation stood on precisely the same ground here. On other points they had their differences; but in asserting the helplessness of man in sin, and the sovereignty of God in grace, they were entirely at one. To all of them, these doctrines were the very life-blood of the Christian faith. . . . To the Reformers, the crucial question was not simply, whether God justifies believers without works of law. It was the broader question, whether sinners are wholly helpless in their sin, and whether God is to be thought of as saving them by free, unconditional, invincible grace, not only justifying them for Christ's sake when they come to faith, but also raising them from the death of sin by His quickening Spirit in order to bring them to faith. Here was the crucial issue: whether God is the author, not merely of justification, but also of faith; whether, in the last analysis, Christianity is a religion of utter reliance on God for salvation

and all things necessary to it, or of self-reliance and self-effort.[1]

In 1610, the followers of Jacob Arminius, a Dutch seminary professor who had died the year before, drew up five articles of faith based on his teachings. These followers, who came to be known as Arminians, then presented their five doctrines to the state of Holland in the form of a Remonstrance (a protest) against the Belgic Confession and the Heidelberg Catechism. The confession and catechism together formed the official expression of the doctrinal positions of the Churches of Holland, which were in close agreement with the teachings of Calvin and the other Reformers. But the Arminians insisted that the teachings within the confession and the catechism on divine sovereignty, human inability, unconditional election or predestination, particular redemption, irresistible grace, and the preservation of the saints be changed to conform to the doctrinal views contained in the Remonstrance.[2]

The beliefs of the Arminians, as expressed in the Remonstrance, were not new. They were a rehashing of the views of Pelagius and Cassian in the fifth and sixth centuries, teachings that had been decreed to be heresy.

A national synod was called to meet in Dort, Holland, in 1618 for the purpose of examining the views of Arminius in light of Scripture. The synod of 111 members from Holland, Germany, Switzerland, England, and Scotland held 154 sessions in a seven-month period. The synod unanimously rejected the teachings of Arminius as being contrary to the Word of God. The members were convinced, however, that a mere rejection was not sufficient. So they developed a biblical response in five chapters that we know today as "the five points of Calvinism."

"Calvinism" has been called a synonym for biblical Christianity. Paul was a Calvinist, Augustine was a Calvinist, and Luther was a Calvinist.

For many years, Calvinistic doctrine was the dominant position among Protestants. In fact, the denominations and groups that were represented in the founding of the United States—Episcopalians, Puritans, Pilgrims, Presbyterians, and Baptists—were all Calvinistic or Reformed in their doctrine. At the time of the American Revolution, an overwhelming majority of the people in the United States were Calvinists.

Today things are substantially different. The doctrines of the Arminians have gained wide acceptance in the modern church. In fact, they are seldom questioned in our day, as the great majority of Christians in the United States hold to some or all of these views. Those who hold the Calvinistic doctrines of the Bible are in the minority.

The next chapter of this book will list the five points of Calvinism and compare them with the five points of Arminianism. Then, in the following five chapters, we will tackle five dilemmas that have kept many in the modern world from accepting and believing the truth that is Calvinism.

Above all else, this will be an exciting exploration of the truth of the sovereignty of God. I have spent a lot of time studying church history, and reading and thinking about divine sovereignty, and I have come to the conclusion that an understanding of this truth is essential if one's faith is to stand up against the world. However, most Christians today do not give much thought to this subject. But if you will approach this journey with an open mind and heart, at the end of this book I believe you will have gone from seeing the relationship between God and man like this:

God   Man

to seeing it more like this:

God   Man

Only when you understand how great, awesome, and powerful God is will you begin to appreciate the sacrifice of Jesus Christ. As Jesus Himself said, "If you abide in my word, you are truly my disciples, and you will know the truth, and the truth will set you free" (John 8:31b–32).

NOTES

1 J. I. Packer, "Historical and Theological Introduction," in Martin Luther, *The Bondage of the Will* (Westwood, N.J.: Fleming H. Revell, 1957), 58–59.

2 David N. Steele and Curtis C. Thomas, *The Five Points of Calvinism: Defined, Defended, Documented* (Phillipsburg, N.J.: P&R Publishing, 1963), 13.

Chapter 2

The Tulip and the Daisy

What are the differences between Calvinism and Arminianism, and what does the Bible teach?

The doctrinal system known as Arminianism has totally or partially taken over most Protestant denominations. This is due not to a latent superiority in Arminianism but mainly to a misunderstanding of Calvinism. For instance, it is sometimes said that Calvinism denies man's responsibility, makes man God's puppet, or removes God's love from the Bible. These statements are not true.

In order to show what Reformed Christians believe and why, this chapter will compare and contrast the doctrinal systems of Calvinism and Arminianism, and provide Scripture references that support the truth. We will look at each of the five points of Calvinism, which are summarized by the acronym TULIP, and the Arminian response. (Arminians also have a flower, the daisy, because their doctrinal system says, in effect, "He loves me, He loves me not.")

In making these comparisons and contrasts, I am heavily indebted to David N. Steele and Curtis C. Thomas, who wrote the small treasure of a book titled *The Five Points of Calvinism: Defined, Defended, Documented.* In addition to their fine explanations of these two doctrinal schools, Steele and Thomas provide even more scriptural support for these doctrines than I am listing in this short overview.

❧

The "T" in TULIP stands for **total depravity**. Steele and Thomas write that this doctrine declares, "Because of the fall, man is unable of himself to savingly believe the gospel. The sinner is dead, blind, and deaf to the things of God; his heart is deceitful and desperately corrupt. His will is not free, it is in bondage to his evil nature, therefore, he will not—indeed he cannot—choose good over evil. Consequently, it takes much more than the Spirit's assistance to bring a sinner to Christ—it takes regeneration by which the Holy Spirit makes the sinner [spiritually] alive and gives him a new nature. Faith is not something man contributes to salvation, but is itself a part of God's gift of salvation."[1]

Arminianism, by contrast, proclaims free will or human ability. Its adherents say that "although human nature was seriously affected by the fall, man has not been left in a state of total spiritual helplessness. . . . Each person possesses a free will, and his eternal destiny depends on how he uses it. . . . The sinner has the power to either cooperate with God's Spirit and be regenerated or resist God's grace and perish. . . . Faith is man's act and precedes the new birth. Faith is the sinner's gift to God; it is man's contribution to salvation."[2]

In summary, the Arminian believes that man is born good and has the ability to choose God. The Calvinist believes that man is born corrupt (dead in his sin), so he must be made alive spiritually before he can do anything of a spiritual nature. Under the Calvinistic doctrinal system, man's depravity is total in extent (though not in degree). In other words, all of man's nature is corrupted by sin, but he is not as evil as he could be.

The basic issue is whether fallen man has the moral ability to incline himself to the things of God without being regenerated first.

Consider these Scripture passages that teach total depravity:

And the LORD God commanded the man, saying, "You may surely eat of every tree of the garden, but of the tree of the knowledge of good and evil you shall not eat, for in the day that you eat of it you shall surely die." (Gen. 2:16–17)

The LORD saw that the wickedness of man was great in the earth, and that every intention of the thoughts of his heart was only evil continually. (Gen. 6:5)

"Who can bring a clean thing out of an unclean? There is not one." (Job 14:4)

Behold, I was brought forth in iniquity, and in sin did my mother conceive me. (Ps. 51:5)

Jesus answered, "Truly, truly, I say to you, unless one is born of water and the Spirit, he cannot enter the kingdom of God. That which is born of the flesh is flesh, and that which is born of the Spirit is spirit. Do not marvel that I said to you, 'You must be born again.'" (John 3:5–7)

"No one can come to me unless the Father who sent me draws him. And I will raise him up on the last day." (John 6:44)

"None is righteous, no, not one; no one understands; no one seeks for God. All have turned aside; together they have become worthless; no one does good, not even one." (Rom. 3:10–12)

For the mind that is set on the flesh is hostile to God, for it does not submit to God's law; indeed, it cannot. Those who are in the flesh cannot please God. (Rom. 8:7–8)

The natural person does not accept the things of the Spirit of God, for they are folly to him, and he is not able to understand them because they are spiritually discerned. (1 Cor. 2:14)

And you were dead in the trespasses and sins in which you once walked, following the course of this world, following the prince of the power of the air, the spirit that is now at work in the sons of disobedience—among whom we all once lived in the passions of our flesh, carrying out the desires of the body and the mind, and were by nature children of wrath, like the rest of mankind. (Eph. 2:1–3)

And you, who were dead in your trespasses and the uncircumcision of your flesh, God made alive together with him, having forgiven us all our trespasses. (Col. 2:13)

❀

The "U" in TULIP stands for **unconditional election**. This doctrine holds that "God's choice of certain individuals unto salvation before the foundation of the world rested solely in His own sovereign will. His choice of particular sinners was not based on any foreseen response or obedience on their part, such as faith, repentance, etc. On the contrary, God gives faith and repentance to each individual whom He selected. These acts are the result, not the cause, of God's choice. . . . God's choice of the sinner, not the sinner's choice of Christ, is the ultimate cause of salvation."[3]

But Arminianism teaches that "God's choice of certain individuals for salvation before the foundation of the world was based upon His foreseeing that they would respond to His call. He selected only those whom He knew would of themselves freely believe the gospel. Election, therefore, was determined by or conditioned on what man would do. The faith which God foresaw and upon which He based His choice was not given to the sinner by God . . . but resulted solely from man's will. . . . The sinner's choice of Christ . . . is the ultimate cause of salvation."[4]

Thus, the Arminian believes that God's choice is based on man's action. The Calvinist, on the other hand, believes that God's choice is based on His divine will.

The doctrine of unconditional election is also known as *predestination*, a word that sends chills up the spines of those who do not understand it. But those who reject this doctrine must ask themselves what kind of a God they want to believe in: a God who is in control of everything or one who is at the mercy of man and his decisions.

Think on these Scripture passages that support uncon-ditional election:

"I will be gracious to whom I will be gracious, and will show mercy on whom I will show mercy." (Ex. 33:19b)

Blessed is the nation whose God is the LORD, the people whom he has chosen as his heritage! (Ps. 33:12)

Our God is in the heavens; he does all that he pleases. (Ps. 115:3)

"No one knows the Father except the Son and anyone to whom the Son chooses to reveal him." (Matt. 11:27b)

"For many are called, but few are chosen." (Matt. 22:14)

"And if the Lord had not cut short the days, no human being would be saved. But for the sake of the elect, whom he chose, he shortened the days." (Mark 13:20)

"I am not speaking of all of you; I know whom I have chosen." (John 13:18a)

"You did not choose me, but I chose you and appointed you that you should go and bear fruit and that your fruit should abide, so that whatever you ask the Father in my name, he may give it to you." (John 15:16)

And when the Gentiles heard this, they began rejoicing and glorifying the word of the Lord, and as many as were appointed to eternal life believed. (Acts 13:48b)

And we know that for those who love God all things work together for good, for those who are called according to his purpose. For those whom he foreknew he also predestined to be conformed to the image of his Son, in order that he might be the firstborn among many brothers. (Rom. 8:28–29)

Though they were not yet born and had done nothing either good or bad—in order that God's purpose of election might continue, not because of works but because of his call—she was told, "The older will serve the younger." As it is written, "Jacob I loved, but Esau I hated." (Rom. 9:11–13)

So then it depends not on human will or exertion, but on God, who has mercy. (Rom. 9:16)

So then he has mercy on whomever he wills, and he hardens whomever he wills. (Rom. 9:18)

He chose us in him before the foundation of the world, that we should be holy and blameless before him. (Eph. 1:4)

He predestined us for adoption through Jesus Christ, according to the purpose of his will. (Eph. 1:5)

God chose you as the firstfruits to be saved, through sanc-
tification by the Spirit and belief in the truth. To this he
called you through our gospel, so that you may obtain the
glory of our Lord Jesus Christ. (2 Thess. 2:13b–14)

Paul, a servant of God and an apostle of Jesus Christ, for
the sake of the faith of God's elect and their knowledge of
the truth, which accords with godliness. (Titus 1:1)

And all who dwell on earth will worship it, everyone
whose name has not been written before the foundation of
the world in the book of life of the Lamb that was slain.
(Rev. 13:8)

The "L" in TULIP is for **limited atonement**, but a better
phrase would be **particular redemption**. This doctrine
states that "Christ's redeeming work was intended to save
the elect only and actually secured salvation for them. His
death was a substitutionary endurance of the penalty of
sin in the place of certain specified sinners. . . . Christ's
redemption secured everything necessary for their salvation, including faith which unites them to Him. The gift
of faith is infallibly applied by the Spirit to all for whom
Christ died, thereby guaranteeing their salvation."[5]

The corresponding Arminian doctrine can be called

general atonement or universal redemption. It holds that "Christ's redeeming work made it possible for everyone to be saved but did not actually secure the salvation of anyone. Although Christ died for all men and for every man, only those who believe in Him are saved. His death enabled God to pardon sinners on the condition that they believe, but it did not actually put away anyone's sins. Christ's redemption becomes effective only if man chooses to accept it."[6]

So the Arminian believes that Christ died for everyone. The Calvinist believes that Christ died only for the elect. Since we know from the Bible that there are people in hell, if Christ did die for everyone, Christ is a failure. As Loraine Boettner has written, the atonement in the Calvinist view "is like a narrow bridge which goes all the way across the stream; for the Arminian it is like a great wide bridge that goes only half-way across."[7] In other words, Calvinism teaches that salvation is complete for some rather than partial for all.

Consider these Scripture passages that uphold limited atonement and teach that God actually accomplished redemption for His people:

> *"She will bear a son, and you shall call his name Jesus, for he will save his people from their sins." (Matt. 1:21)*

"For this is my blood of the covenant, which is poured out for many for the forgiveness of sins." (Matt. 26:28)

"I am the good shepherd; I know my own and my own know me, just as the Father knows me and I know the Father; and I lay down my life for the sheep." (John 10:14–15)

"You have given him authority over all flesh, to give eternal life to all whom you have given him." (John 17:2)

"I am praying for them. I am not praying for the world but for those whom you have given me, for they are yours. All mine are yours, and yours are mine, and I am glorified in them." (John 17:9–10)

"Father, I desire that they also, whom you have given me, may be with me where I am, to see my glory that you have given me because you loved me before the foundation of the world." (John 17:24)

For if while we were enemies we were reconciled to God by the death of his Son, much more, now that we are reconciled, shall we be saved by his life. (Rom. 5:10)

Grace to you and peace from God our Father and the Lord Jesus Christ, who gave himself for our sins to deliver us from the present evil age, according to the will of our God and Father. (Gal. 1:3–4)

Christ redeemed us from the curse of the law by becoming a curse for us. (Gal. 3:13a)

Who gave himself for us to redeem us from all lawlessness and to purify for himself a people for his own possession who are zealous for good works. (Titus 2:14)

He himself bore our sins in his body on the tree, that we might die to sin and live to righteousness. By his wounds you have been healed. (1 Peter 2:24)

And they sang a new song, saying, "Worthy are you to take the scroll and to open its seals, for you were slain, and by your blood you ransomed people for God from every tribe and language and people and nation." (Rev. 5:9)

The "I" in TULIP stands for **irresistible grace**. This doctrine asserts that, "In addition to the outward general call to salvation which is made to everyone who hears the gospel, the Holy Spirit extends to the elect a special inward call that inevitably brings them to salvation. The external call (which is made to all without distinction) can be, and often is, rejected; whereas the internal call (which is made only to the elect) cannot be refused; it always results in conversion. . . . The Spirit graciously causes the elect sinner to cooperate, to believe, to repent, to come freely and willingly to Christ. God's grace . . . never fails to result in the salvation of those to whom it is extended."[8]

By contrast, the Arminian believes in resistible grace. This theological school teaches that "The Spirit calls inwardly all who are called outwardly by the gospel invitation; He does all that He can to bring every sinner to salvation. But inasmuch as man is free, he can successfully resist the Spirit's call. . . . Thus, man's free will limits the Spirit in the application of Christ's saving work. The Holy Spirit can only draw to Christ those who allow Him to have His way with them. Until the sinner responds, the Spirit cannot give life. God's grace, therefore, is not invincible; it can be, and often is, resisted and thwarted by man."[9]

In summary, the Arminian believes that God knocks on the door to man's heart and man decides to answer or not. The Calvinist believes that anyone whom the Holy Spirit regenerates is saved. This is because God's grace works effectually only on the elect. He never wastes His effort or is frustrated in His design. If you are one of God's elect, He will bring you to Himself sometime in your life. His desire for you will never be quenched until you are one of His.

Ponder these Scripture passages that teach irresistible grace:

"I will give you a new heart, and a new spirit I will put within you. And I will remove the heart of stone from your flesh and give you a heart of flesh. And I will put my Spirit within you, and cause you to walk in my statutes and be careful to obey my rules." (Ezek. 36:26–27)

In that same hour he rejoiced in the Holy Spirit and said, "I thank you, Father, Lord of heaven and earth, that you have hidden these things from the wise and understanding and revealed them to little children; yes, Father; for such was your gracious will." (Luke 10:21)

"For as the Father raises the dead and gives them life, so also the Son gives life to whom he will." (John 5:21)

"All that the Father gives me will come to me, and whoever comes to me I will never cast out. . . . No one can come to me unless the Father who sent me draws him. And I will raise him up on the last day. It is written in the Prophets, 'And they will all be taught by God.' Everyone who has heard and learned from the Father comes to me." (John 6:37, 44–45)

One who heard us was a woman named Lydia, from the city of Thyatira, a seller of purple goods, who was a worshiper of God. The Lord opened her heart to pay attention to what was said by Paul. (Acts 16:14)

And those whom he predestined he also called, and those whom he called he also justified, and those whom he justified he also glorified. (Rom. 8:30)

But when he who had set me apart before I was born, and who called me by his grace, was pleased to reveal his Son to me, in order that I might preach him among the Gentiles, I did not immediately consult with anyone. (Gal. 1:15–16)

[I pray] that the God of our Lord Jesus Christ, the Father of glory, may give you a spirit of wisdom and of revelation in the knowledge of him, having the eyes of your hearts enlightened, that you may know what is the hope to which he has called you. (Eph. 1:17–18a)

For by grace you have been saved through faith. And this is not your own doing; it is the gift of God, not a result of works, so that no one may boast. (Eph. 2:8–9)

There is one body and one Spirit—just as you were called to the one hope that belongs to your call. (Eph. 4:4)

Therefore he is the mediator of a new covenant, so that those who are called may receive the promised eternal inheritance. (Heb. 9:15a)

But you are a chosen race, a royal priesthood, a holy nation, a people for his own possession, that you may proclaim the excellencies of him who called you out of darkness into his marvelous light. (1 Peter 2:9)

And we know that the Son of God has come and has given us understanding, so that we may know him who is true; and we are in him who is true, in his Son Jesus Christ. He is the true God and eternal life. (1 John 5:20)

The "P" in TULIP is for **the perseverance of the saints**. For a Calvinist, this is the culmination of an orderly system, for this doctrine affirms that "All who were chosen by God, redeemed by Christ, and given faith by the Spirit are eternally saved. They are kept in faith by the power of Almighty God and thus persevere to the end."[10]

By contrast, the Arminian system allows for the possibility of a fall from grace. It holds that "those who believe and are truly saved can lose their salvation by failing to keep up their faith, etc."[11]

In summary, the Arminian believes that a person can become a Christian and then fall away. The Calvinist believes that once a person is truly saved, he is always saved, for he is kept in faith by God.

What about those who attend church for years, give of their time and resources, and show outward signs of faith and repentance, only to end their lives in rebellion and sin? The Calvinist does not believe that such people have fallen from grace, but that they were never saved! Jesus said in Matthew 7:21–23: "'Not everyone who says to me "Lord, Lord," will enter the kingdom of heaven, but the one who does the will of my Father who is in heaven. On that day many will say to me, "Lord, Lord, did we not prophesy in your name, and cast out demons in your name, and do many mighty works in your name?" And then will I declare to them, "I never knew you; depart from me, you workers of lawlessness."'"

Meditate on these Scripture passages that undergird the doctrine of the perseverance of the saints:

"For the mountains may depart and the hills be removed, but my steadfast love shall not depart from you, and my covenant of peace shall not be removed," says the LORD, who has compassion on you. (Isa. 54:10)

"What do you think? If a man has a hundred sheep and one of them has gone astray, does he not leave the ninety-nine on the mountains and go in search of the one that went astray? And if he finds it, truly, I say to you, he rejoices over it more than over the ninety-nine that never went astray. So it is not the will of my Father who is in heaven that one of these little ones should perish." (Matt. 18:12–14)

Whoever believes in the Son has eternal life. (John 3:36a)

"Truly, truly, I say to you, whoever hears my word and believes him who sent me has eternal life. He does not come into judgment, but has passed from death to life." (John 5:24)

"Truly, truly, I say to you, whoever believes has eternal life." (John 6:47)

"My sheep hear my voice, and I know them, and they follow me. I give them eternal life, and they will never perish, and no one will snatch them out of my hand. My Father, who has given them to me, is greater than all, and no one is able to snatch them out of the Father's hand. I and the Father are one." (John 10:27–30)

Those whom he predestined he also called, and those whom he called he also justified, and those whom he justified he also glorified. (Rom. 8:30)

For I am sure that neither death nor life, nor angels nor rulers, nor things present nor things to come, nor powers, nor height nor depth, nor anything else in all creation, will be able to separate us from the love of God in Christ Jesus our Lord. (Rom. 8:38–39)

You are not lacking in any spiritual gift, as you wait for the revealing of our Lord Jesus Christ, who will sustain you to the end, guiltless in the day of our Lord Jesus Christ. God is faithful, by whom you were called into the fellowship of his Son, Jesus Christ our Lord. (1 Cor. 1:7–9)

He who raised the Lord Jesus will raise us also with Jesus and bring us with you into his presence. . . . For this slight momentary affliction is preparing for us an eternal weight of glory beyond all comparison. (2 Cor. 4:14, 17)

And do not grieve the Holy Spirit of God, by whom you were sealed for the day of redemption. (Eph. 4:30)

For you have died, and your life is hidden with Christ in God. When Christ who is your life appears, then you also will appear with him in glory. (Col. 3:3–4)

The Lord will rescue me from every evil deed and bring me safely into his heavenly kingdom. To him be the glory forever and ever. Amen. (2 Tim. 4:18)

We might summarize the Calvinistic view of redemption like so:

- The Father elects. That is, He chooses those to be saved.
- The Son redeems. He pays the price for the elect.

- The Spirit applies. He gives the benefits of redemption to the elect.

Some people call themselves three- or four-point Calvinists, and many Arminians believe in the perseverance of the saints. However, these partial Calvinists are inconsistent. We cannot choose which points of Calvinism we will accept and reject, since each is part of a system that falls apart if it is not whole.

NOTES

1 David N. Steele and Curtis C. Thomas, *The Five Points of Calvinism: Defined, Defended, Documented* (Phillipsburg, N.J.: P&R Publishing, 1963), 16.

2 Ibid., 16.

3 Ibid., 16–17

4 Ibid., 16–17

5 Ibid., 17

6 Ibid., 17

7 Loraine Boettner, from *Predestination*, as quoted in Steele and Thomas, *The Five Points of Calvinism: Defined, Defended, Documented*, 40.

8 Steele and Thomas, *The Five Points of Calvinism: Defined, Defended, Documented*, 18.

9 Ibid., 18.

10 Ibid., 18.

11 Ibid., 18.

Chapter 3

Dilemma one— Responsibility

If God is in complete control of everything, to the point of predetermining all human actions, how can man be held accountable for what he does?

The difference between Calvinism and Arminianism is sometimes stated in this way: Calvinists, who are also known as Reformed Christians, believe that God is sovereign and has predetermined everything that has happened and will happen in this world, while Arminians believe man has the ability to make his own choices and is not forced to do anything.

In actuality, both of the above statements are true. God

is sovereign and man *is* able to make choices for which he is responsible. This so-called contradiction, which is one of the highest mysteries of the Scriptures, is one of the fundamental truths of the Reformed faith.

The difference cited above, then, is based on a misunderstanding of Calvinism. The true distinction between Calvinism and Arminianism is that Calvinists believe in *both* God's sovereignty and man's responsibility, while Arminians say that because God's sovereignty and man's responsibility appear contradictory, only one can be right. They choose the one that seems logical from man's perspective—human free choice.

How can Calvinists affirm both God's sovereignty and human responsibility? These twin truths seem totally irreconcilable. If God has predetermined everything that happens, we wonder how our decisions can mean anything. And since we know we make decisions, we wonder how God can be said to be sovereign.

We must go to Scripture to find the resolution to this apparent contradiction. We'll start with Exodus.

During the account of the plagues God brought upon Egypt, the Bible repeatedly says that Pharaoh hardened his heart and refused to let his Israelite slaves go (Ex. 7:13, 14, 22; 8:15, etc.). In other words, Pharaoh chose to disobey God of his own free will. However, the Lord had planned it that way, which is why the Bible also says God hardened Pharaoh's heart (Ex. 4:21; 7:3; 9:12, etc.).

At first glance, this doesn't make sense. But the Bible tells us in at least two other places that God controls the leaders of nations. Proverbs 21:1 says, "The king's heart is a stream of water in the hand of the LORD; he turns it wherever he will." And Daniel 2:20–21 says, "'Blessed be the name of God forever and ever, to whom belong wisdom and might. He changes times and seasons; he removes kings and sets up kings; he gives wisdom to the wise and knowledge to those who have understanding.'"

But God's control of kings is just one aspect of His authority. He is sovereign over His universe. He determines *everything* that is going to happen, both to kings and to you and me. Consider these verses that speak of God's sovereignty:

"I know that you can do all things, and that no purpose of yours can be thwarted." (Job 42:2)

The LORD has established his throne in the heavens, and his kingdom rules over all. (Ps. 103:19)

In your book were written, every one of them, the days that were formed for me, when as yet there were none of them. (Ps. 139:16b)

The LORD of hosts has sworn: "As I have planned, so shall it be, and as I have purposed, so shall it stand." (Isa. 14:24)

"I am God, and there is none like me, declaring the end from the beginning and from ancient times things not yet done, saying, 'My counsel shall stand, and I will accomplish all my purpose.'" (Isa. 46:9b–10)

"So shall my word be that goes out from my mouth; it shall not return to me empty, but it shall accomplish that which I purpose, and shall succeed in the thing for which I sent it." (Isa. 55:11)

For by grace you have been saved through faith. And this is not your own doing; it is the gift of God, not a result of works, so that no one may boast. (Eph. 2:8–9)

Clearly, then, Scripture shows that God is sovereign. But we all know we have free will. If you decide right now to shut this book because you do not like what you are reading, you will be doing so of your own free will. No one will be forcing you to do it. Yet if you do it, it will be because God predetermined that you would. How can this be?

Wayne Grudem explains that this is the doctrine of concurrence. He defines it this way: "The fact that God cooperates with created things in every action, directing their distinctive properties to cause them to act as they do."[1]

With this understanding, it is possible to affirm that, in every event, both God's sovereign will and man's human will are operative. God brings His will to pass, not by canceling the will of the creature, but by working *through* the will of the creature. God's will is the "primary cause"; He works behind the scenes from the beginning of time to plan and initiate everything that happens. Man's will is the "secondary cause"; it carries out events in a manner consistent with God's will.

For example, when God wishes to save a sinner, He does not strike the individual with "divine lightning." Rather, He uses a godly man to witness to that individual. Man, the "secondary cause," appears to be the *only* cause, but in reality God is the "primary cause," for He works in the evangelist's heart to give him the desire to witness and in the recipient's heart to allow him to accept the truth he is receiving.

Grudem adds:

God's providential direction as an unseen, behind-the-scenes "primary cause," should not lead us to deny the reality of our choices and actions. Again and again Scripture affirms that we really do cause events to happen. We are significant and we are responsible. We do have choices, and these are real choices that bring about real results. . . .

God causes all things that happen, but . . . he does so in such a way that he somehow upholds our ability to make *willing, responsible* choices that have *real and eternal results,* and for which we are *held accountable.* Exactly how God combines his providential control with our willing and significant choices, Scripture does not explain to us. But rather than deny one aspect or the other (simply because we cannot explain how both can be true), we should accept both in an attempt to be faithful to the teaching of all of Scripture.[2]

One of the clearest examples of concurrence in Scripture occurs in the story of Jonah. The author of this biblical book tells us that the men on the ship threw Jonah into the sea and simultaneously affirms that it was God who threw him overboard. God's providential direction of events did not coerce the sailors to act against their wills. They were unaware that He was influencing their behavior and actually prayed for His forgiveness. God chose to act through the choices of these real human beings, men who were morally accountable for their actions, in order to bring about His plan for the salvation of Nineveh. He caused them to choose to do what they did, but they did it willingly with no knowledge of His influence.

To reinforce the truth that the Bible teaches both God's sovereignty and man's responsibility, I want to look at three additional verses that talk about both doctrines.

Proverbs 16:9 says, "The heart of man plans his way, but the LORD establishes his steps." Here God affirms that we human beings plan out our lives and make our decisions, but He already has determined what will occur.

Proverbs 19:21 reads, "Many are the plans in the mind of a man, but it is the purpose of the LORD that will stand." Here God again says that man makes his plans according to his own desires, but those plans are perfectly matched with God's purposes.

Finally, in John 6:37, Jesus says, "'All that the Father gives me will come to me, and whoever comes to me I will never cast out.'" This is my favorite verse in the Bible, because in it we see the dual truths of God's election of His people and the freedom for anyone who so desires to come to Him and be one of His.

"All that the Father gives me" refers to those elect individuals whom God has chosen from the foundation of the world to believe in Him. "Will come to me" means that, sometime in their lives, those elect individuals will choose to believe in Christ as their Savior and their Lord. "And whoever comes to me" means that the invitation is open to anyone to believe in Christ. "I will never cast out" means that anyone who does come to Christ will be saved.

But again, how can this be? How can the twin truths of God's sovereignty and man's responsibility appear side by side in one verse of Scripture?

God gives us a fabulous passage that answers this question. In what I believe to be the most powerful passage in the Bible, God answers our dilemma. In Romans 9:14–24, we read:

> *What shall we say then? Is there injustice on God's part? By no means! For he says to Moses, "I will have mercy on whom I have mercy, and I will have compassion on whom I have compassion." So then it depends not on human will or exertion, but on God, who has mercy. For the Scripture says to Pharaoh, "For this very purpose I have raised you up, that I might show my power in you, and that my name might be proclaimed in all the earth." So he has mercy on whomever he wills, and he hardens whomever he wills.*
>
> *You will say to me then, "Why does he still find fault? For who can resist his will?" But who are you, O man, to answer back to God? Shall what is molded say to its*

molder, "Why have you made me like this?" Has the pot-
ter no right over the clay, to make out of the same lump
one vessel for honored use and another for dishonorable
use? What if God, desiring to show his wrath and to make
known his power, has endured with much patience ves-
sels of wrath prepared for destruction, in order to make
known the riches of his glory for vessels of mercy, which he
has prepared beforehand for glory—even us whom he has
called, not from the Jews only but also from the Gentiles?

Did this sink in? In Paul's hypothetical example, man is saying what the Arminians say: It's not fair and it does not make sense. God's basic response is this: "Who do you think you are? I am God. You are man. There is a big difference."

So the answer to the question of how God can harden Pharaoh's heart and Pharaoh can yet make his own deci-sions is simple—God set it up that way. He is God, so He can do anything He wants. Just because our finite minds cannot comprehend something He does has nothing to do with the reality of it.

While we are free from our perspective, we must real-ize that absolute "freedom"—total freedom from God's control—is simply not possible in a world providentially sustained and directed by God Himself. Human freedom is real, but it is everywhere limited by God's freedom. It is God who is sovereign, not man. This sovereignty is never limited by human freedom. Rather, human freedom is always limited by God's sovereignty.

The simple fact of the matter is that no event falls outside of God's providence; if it did, He would not be God. It is because Paul knew that God is sovereign over all and works His purposes in every event that happens that he could declare that "for those who love God all things work together for good, for those who are called according to his purpose" (Rom. 8:28).

Because He is both God and man, Jesus knows this from both perspectives. On the night before His crucifixion, He prayed, "'Father, if you are willing, remove this cup from me. Nevertheless, not my will, but yours, be done'" (Luke 22:42). All the actions of all the participants in Jesus' crucifixion had been "predestined" by God. Yet the apostles never blame God for the actions that resulted from the willing choices of sinful men. Peter discussed this at Pentecost in Acts 2:23, when he stated, "'This Jesus, delivered up according to the definite plan and foreknowledge of God, you crucified and killed by the hands of lawless men.'" God did not force these men to act against their wills. They did what they wanted to do and were totally responsible for their actions. God, however, is so awesome that He was able to bring about His eternal plan for the salvation of mankind through the willing choices of the Jewish mob.

Where does this leave us? We are now beginning to see that God is sovereign over all things, even the minutest details of the universe, but that at the same time we all have the ability to choose what we desire. Our problem is that we desire sin. Thus, we are left with one thought: Our God is altogether worthy of our worship!

God is much greater than we can possibly imagine. A deity so powerful that He can allow His creatures to make free choices, yet determine from the foundation of time what those choices will be, leaves us in total awe. This truth should make us want to fall on our knees in total praise and submission to Him.

At the same time, this truth should bring tears of thankfulness to our eyes. It is nearly incomprehensible that a God this powerful loved you and me enough not only to choose us from the beginning of time, but also to work all things together for our good. Only an all-powerful God could do this.

To show the dual truths of God's sovereignty and man's responsibility in the Scriptures, here are some verses that describe each:

God's sovereignty:

Therefore David blessed the LORD in the presence of all the assembly. And David said : "Blessed are you, O LORD, the God of Israel our father, forever and ever. Yours, O LORD, is the greatness and the power and the glory and the victory and the majesty, for all that is in the heavens and in the earth is yours. Yours is the kingdom, O LORD, and you are exalted as head above all. Both riches and honor come from you, and you rule over all. In your hand are power and might, and in your hand it is to make great and to give strength to all." (1 Chron. 29:10–12)

Then Job answered the LORD and said: "I know that you can do all things, and that no purpose of yours can be thwarted." (Job 42:1–2)

Our God is in the heavens; he does all that he pleases. (Ps. 115:3)

Whatever the LORD pleases, he does, in heaven and on earth, in the seas and all deeps. (Ps. 135:6)

The LORD of hosts has sworn: "As I have planned, so shall it be, and as I have purposed, so shall it stand. . . ." For the LORD of hosts has purposed, and who will annul it? His hand is stretched out, and who will turn it back. (Isa. 14:24–27)

"'Ah, Lord GOD! It is you who has made the heavens and the earth by your great power and by your outstretched arm! Nothing is too hard for you.'" (Jer. 32:17)

All the inhabitants of the earth are accounted as nothing, and he does according to his will among the host of heaven and among the inhabitants of the earth. (Dan. 4:35a)

"Then the King will say to those on his right, 'Come, you who are blessed by my Father, inherit the kingdom prepared for you from the foundation of the world.'" (Matt. 25:34)

"No one can come to me unless the Father who sent me draws him." (John 6:44a)

"You did not choose me, but I chose you and appointed you that you should go and bear fruit." (John 15:16a)

"And he made from one man every nation of mankind to live on all the face of the earth, having determined allotted periods and the boundaries of their dwelling place." (Acts 17:26)

And we know that for those who love God all things work together for good, for those who are called according to his purpose. (Rom. 8:28)

For those whom he foreknew he also predestined to be conformed to the image of his Son, in order that he might be the firstborn among many brothers. And those whom he predestined he also called, and those whom he called he also justified, and those whom he justified he also glorified. (Rom. 8:29–30)

For he says to Moses, "I will have mercy on whom I have mercy, and I will have compassion on whom I have compassion." So then it depends not on human will or exertion, but on God, who has mercy. (Rom. 9:15–16)

He chose us in him before the foundation of the world, that we should be holy and blameless before him. In love he predestined us for adoption through Jesus Christ, according to the purpose of his will. (Eph. 1:4–5)

God chose you as the firstfruits to be saved, through sanctification by the Spirit and belief in the truth. (2 Thess. 2:13b)

Man's responsibility:

Tell the righteous that it shall be well with them, for they shall eat the fruit of their deeds. (Isa. 3:10)

"Again, when a wicked person turns away from the wickedness he has committed and does what is just and right, he shall save his life. Because he considered and turned away from all the transgressions that he had committed, he shall surely live; he shall not die." (Ezek. 18:27–28)

"When the righteous turns from his righteousness and does injustice, he shall die for it. And when the wicked turns from his wickedness and does what is just and right, he shall live by this." (Ezek. 33:18–19)

"The one who endures to the end will be saved." (Matt. 24:13)

"Whoever believes in him is not condemned, but whoever does not believe is condemned already, because he has not believed in the name of the only Son of God." (John 3:18)

"Whoever hears my word and believes him who sent me has eternal life. He does not come into judgment, but has passed from death to life." (John 5:24)

"The one who rejects me and does not receive my words has a judge; the word that I have spoken will judge him on the last day." (John 12:48)

"Repent and be baptized every one of you in the name of Jesus Christ for the forgiveness of your sins, and you will receive the gift of the Holy Spirit." (Acts 2:38)

He will render to each one according to his works: to those who by patience in well-doing seek for glory and honor and immortality, he will give eternal life; but for those who are self-seeking and do not obey the truth,

> *but obey unrighteousness, there will be wrath and fury.*
> *(Rom. 2:6–8)*

> *Let not sin therefore reign in your mortal bodies, to make*
> *you obey their passions. (Rom. 6:12)*

> *If you confess with your mouth that Jesus is Lord and*
> *believe in your heart that God raised him from the dead,*
> *you will be saved. (Rom. 10:9)*

> *The fruit of the Spirit is love, joy, peace, patience, kind-*
> *ness, goodness, faithfulness, gentleness, self-control. (Gal.*
> *5:22–23a)*

> *So then, brothers, stand firm and hold to the traditions*
> *that you were taught by us. (2 Thess. 2:15a)*

These are just some of the verses in Scripture that point out either God's sovereignty or man's responsibility. Clearly we are free beings who make our own decisions every moment of every day. And yet, God is in complete control of His creation and has predetermined everything that comes to pass. What an awesome God in which to place our hope and trust.

NOTES

1 Wayne Grudem, *Systematic Theology* (Grand Rapids, Mich.: Zondervan, 1994), 317.

2 Ibid., 321.

Chapter 4

Dilemma Two— Motivation

If we are saved by grace and not by works, why should we do anything good? What purpose do good works serve? Are there rewards in heaven for what we do here on earth?

The followers of every religion other than Christianity (and even of some mixed-up forms of the Christian faith) hope to earn their way into the afterlife or into earthly happiness by the things they do in this life. For example:

- Radical Muslims become suicide bombers to fight for Allah and earn a ticket to paradise.

- Young Mormon men take two years of their lives to call on people door to door to fulfill a "work requirement."
- Roman Catholics, equating church law and practices with Scripture, attempt to follow decrees of the church in an effort to earn their position with God.
- Misguided Christians donate to religious groups under the misconception that these gifts will assure blessings on this earth and salvation in the afterlife.
- Fundamentalist Christians strive to do good deeds and avoid bad deeds so as to earn favor with God. Their churches often add requirements that are not in the Bible, such as prohibitions against playing cards or bowling, in a legalistic approach to encourage people to live good lives.

Calvinists, of course, understand that salvation is entirely of God and is not influenced by our good works:

For by grace you have been saved through faith. And this is not your own doing; it is the gift of God, not a result of works, so that no one may boast. For we are his workmanship, created in Christ Jesus for good works, which God prepared beforehand, that we should walk in them. (Eph. 2:8–10)

He saved us, not because of works done by us in righteousness, but according to his own mercy, by the washing of regeneration and renewal of the Holy Spirit, whom he poured out on us richly through Jesus Christ our Savior, so that being justified by his grace we might become heirs according to the hope of eternal life. The saying is trustworthy, and I want you to insist on these things, so that those who have believed in God may be careful to devote themselves to good works. These things are excellent and profitable for people. (Titus 3:5–8)

These passages make it clear that our works contribute nothing to our salvation. The work of redemption was accomplished by Christ alone.

However, this understanding can leave Reformed Christians inadequately motivated to perform good works. If we believe that we do not need to do good works to earn our salvation, what is our motivation for living as God commands?

I believe that Scripture gives us four main reasons to do good works even after we are convinced that we are saved by grace alone. None of these reasons can be found in the world or in any other religion.

First, we should do good works because God asks us to. The Bible is filled with statements from God telling His people to behave or live in a certain manner. As Christians, that is all the motivation we should need. If our Creator tells us to do something, we should do it.

We could look at any number of passages that deal with this subject, but we will focus on three biblical books: Matthew, Galatians, and James. Jesus' Sermon on the Mount, recorded in Matthew 5–7, is filled with instructions on how we are to live. One excellent summary is found in 5:14–16: "'You are the light of the world. A city set on a hill cannot be hidden. Nor do people light a lamp and put it under a basket, but on a stand, and it gives light to all in the house. In the same way, let your light shine before others, so that they may see your good works and give glory to your Father who is in heaven.'"

The other two books that I have chosen, Galatians and James, have long been thought by some to contradict each other. Here is the dilemma: Paul says in Galatians 3:11, "Now it is evident that no one is justified before God by the law, for 'The righteous shall live by faith.'" Then we have James 2:24, which says, "You see that a person is justified by works and not by faith alone." At first glance, these verses appear contradictory, but they are not. Paul and James are in complete agreement. Both are saying that anyone who is truly a Christian will do good works, and if he does not do good works, he has never been saved by faith.

Let's look at some other verses from Galatians and James that call us to do good works so as to please our Father in heaven:

For you were called to freedom, brothers. Only do not use your freedom as an opportunity for the flesh, but through love serve one another. For the whole law is fulfilled in one word: "You shall love your neighbor as yourself." (Gal. 5:13–14)

But I say, walk by the Spirit, and you will not gratify the desires of the flesh. (Gal. 5:16)

Bear one another's burdens, and so fulfill the law of Christ. (Gal. 6:2)

And let us not grow weary of doing good, for in due season we will reap, if we do not give up. So then, as we have opportunity, let us do good to everyone, and especially to those who are of the household of faith. (Gal. 6:9–10)

Know this, my beloved brothers: Let every person be quick to hear, slow to speak, slow to anger; for the anger of man does not produce the righteousness that God requires. Therefore put away all filthiness and rampant wickedness and receive with meekness the implanted word, which is able to save your souls. But be doers of the word, and not hearers only, deceiving yourselves. For if anyone is a hearer of the word and not a doer, he is like a man who looks intently at his natural face in a mirror. For he looks at himself and goes away and at once forgets what he was like. But the one who looks into the perfect law, the law of liberty, and perseveres, being no hearer who forgets but a doer who acts, will be blessed in his doing. If anyone thinks he is religious and does not bridle his tongue but deceives his heart, this person's religion is worthless. Religion that is pure and undefiled before God, the Father, is this: to visit orphans and widows in their affliction, and to keep oneself unstained from the world. (James 1:19–27)

If you really fulfill the royal law according to the Scripture, "You shall love your neighbor as yourself," you are doing well. (James 2:8)

So speak and so act as those who are to be judged under the law of liberty. (James 2:12)

These verses make it clear that God expects good works to mark the lives of His redeemed people.

Second, we should do good works out of appreciation for what God has done for us. Unfortunately, this motivation does not always compel us as it should. It is easier for us to do something because we think we are going to get a reward for it rather than because we want to express thankfulness for what someone else has done for us.

I know that if I say to one of my children, "Would you please mow the yard out of thankfulness for all the food and lodging that you are receiving?" I will get a less-enthusiastic

response than if I say "Would you mow the yard for $20?"
The difference is a reflection of our sinful human natures.
We are much more motivated do good deeds to suppos-
edly earn our way to heaven than to show appreciation for
Christ's death on the cross for us.

God wants us to regard Him as our heavenly "Father,"
a loving being who has chosen us to be His sons and followers. Romans 8:14–17a says: "For all who are led by the Spirit
of God are sons of God. For you did not receive the spirit
of slavery to fall back into fear, but you have received the
Spirit of adoption as sons, by whom we cry, 'Abba! Father!'
The Spirit himself bears witness with our spirit that we are
children of God, and if children, then heirs—heirs of God
and fellow heirs with Christ." As sons of God, we need to
live in appreciation for that blessed relationship and try to
do good works out of a thankful heart.

Consider also 1 Corinthians 6:19b–20: "You are not
your own, for you were bought with a price. So glorify God
in your body." Here again we are reminded that God has
done something spectacular for us. What more motivation
do we need to attempt to please Him and live the Christian
life that the Bible describes?

Third, we should do good works out of an intelligent
fear of the Lord. Proverbs 1:7 says, "The fear of the LORD
is the beginning of knowledge; fools despise wisdom and

instruction." We should have a healthy apprehension about how God will react if we do not practice obedience. While we like to talk about the love of God, the Bible actually has more to say about His wrath. That wrath is mentioned in some of the following verses, which make it very clear that we need to live in a healthy fear of God that encourages us to do good works:

> "Gather the people to me, that I may let them hear my words, so that they may learn to fear me all the days that they live on the earth, and that they may teach their children so." (Deut. 4:10b)

> "Now this is the commandment, the statutes and the rules that the LORD your God commanded me to teach you, that you may do them in the land to which you are going over, to possess it, that you may fear the LORD your God, you and your son and your son's son, by keeping all his statutes and his commandments, which I command you, all the days of your life, and that your days may be long." (Deut. 6:1–2)

> "Now therefore fear the LORD and serve him in sincerity and in faithfulness." (Josh. 24:14a)

> "And he said to man, 'Behold, the fear of the LORD, that is wisdom, and to turn away from evil is understanding.'" (Job 28:28)

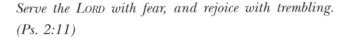

Serve the LORD with fear, and rejoice with trembling. (Ps. 2:11)

Oh, how abundant is your goodness, which you have stored up for those who fear you. (Ps. 31:19a)

For as high as the heavens are above the earth, so great is his steadfast love toward those who fear him. (Ps. 103:11)

Blessed is everyone who fears the LORD, who walks in his ways! (Ps. 128:1)

Fear God and keep his commandments, for this is the whole duty of man. (Eccl. 12:13b)

"And do not fear those who kill the body but cannot kill the soul. Rather fear him who can destroy both soul and body in hell." (Matt. 10:28)

"In every nation anyone who fears him and does what is right is acceptable to him." (Acts 10:35)

For we must all appear before the judgment seat of Christ, so that each one may receive what is due for what he has done in the body, whether good or evil. (2 Cor. 5:10)

Do you see the active verbs in these quotes: "serve," "turn away," "rejoice," "walk," "keep," and "do"? Christianity is not a passive religion. We are to be actively doing good works that please God. And one of the primary reasons for doing them is to avoid the wrath of the almighty and righteous God on our lives.

Hebrews 12:5–6 (a quotation of Proverbs 3:11–12) says: "'My son, do not regard lightly the discipline of the Lord, nor be weary when reproved by him. For the Lord disciplines the one he loves, and chastises every son whom he receives.'" God will change us and mold us into the people He wants us to be. However, we should strive to become those people voluntarily rather than wait for God to force us to see the right path through His perfect discipline.

Our goal in the world, our "chief end," as the Westminster Shorter Catechism puts it, is to "glorify God and enjoy him forever." Every good work that we do in this world is a form of worship that glorifies God and helps to mold our lives in conformity to His will. The fear of the Lord helps to motivate us to live a godly life, triumphing over our sinful natures.

The fourth and final reason we should do good works may surprise you. It surprised me when I first realized it. It is to store up for ourselves rewards in heaven.

In his book *Now, That's a Good Question!* R. C. Sproul considers the question many of you may be asking: "Are there gradations in heaven whereby one Christian, as a result of a lifetime of good works, has a higher rank or better quality of existence . . . than someone who just squeaks through at his last breath?" He answers this question as follows:

> This may come as a surprise to many people, but I would answer that question with an emphatic yes. There are degrees of reward that are given in heaven. I'm surprised that this answer surprises so many people. I think there's a reason Christians are shocked when I say there are various levels of heaven as well as gradations of severity of punishment in hell.
>
> We owe much of this confusion to the Protestant emphasis on the doctrine of justification by faith alone. We hammer away at that doctrine, teaching emphatically that a person does not get to heaven through his good works. Our good works give us no merit whatsoever, and the only way we can possibly enter heaven is by faith in Christ, whose merits are imputed to us. We emphasize this doctrine to the extent that people conclude good works are insignificant and have no bearing at all upon the Christian's future life.
>
> The way historic Protestantism has spelled it out is that the only way we get into heaven is through

the work of Christ, but we are promised rewards in heaven *according to our works.* Saint Augustine said that it's only by the grace of God that we ever do anything even approximating a good work, and none of our works are good enough to demand that God reward them. The fact that God has decided to grant rewards on the basis of obedience or disobedience is what Augustine called God's crowning his own works within us. If a person has been faithful in many things through many years, then he will be acknowledged by his Master, who will say to him, "Well done, thou good and faithful servant." The one who squeaks in at the last moment has precious little good works for which he can expect reward.

I think the gap between tier one and tier ten in heaven is infinitesimal compared to the gap in getting there or not getting there at all. Somebody put it this way: Everybody's cup in heaven is full, but not everybody in heaven has the same size cup. Again, it may be surprising to people, but I'd say there are at least twenty-five occasions where the New Testament clearly teaches that we will be granted rewards according to our works. Jesus frequently holds out the reward motif as the carrot in front of the horse—"great will be your reward in heaven" if you do this or that. We are called to work, to store up treasures for ourselves in heaven, even as the wicked, as Paul tells us in Romans, "treasure up wrath against the day of wrath."[1]

Likewise, in his book titled *The Bible on the Life Hereafter*, William Hendriksen writes:

"But surely in heaven we shall all be equal," says someone. I answer, yes, in the sense that all who enter there will have been sinners who are then in the state of having been "saved by grace." All, moreover, will owe their salvation equally to the sovereign love of God. And the goal for all will be the same, to glorify God and enjoy Him forever. Nevertheless, there will be inequalities, differences, degrees of reward, and in hell degrees of woe. Scripture teaches this doctrine of degrees of glory. When Jesus comes to reward His servants, one of these faithful ones will in the end have ten talents, another four talents. There will be those in the life hereafter who will receive a reward, which others, though saved, will not receive, that is, not in equal measure. Are there not differences among the angels? Is every angel an archangel?[2]

These statements from Sproul and Hendriksen have strong scriptural support. Consider these passages:

But because of your hard and impenitent heart, you are storing up wrath for yourself on the day of wrath when God's righteous judgment will be revealed. He will render to each one according to his works: to those who by patience in well-doing seek for glory and honor and immortality, he will give eternal life; but for those who are self-seeking and do not obey the truth, but obey unrighteousness, there will be wrath and fury. (Rom. 2:5–8)

According to the grace of God given to me, like a skilled master builder I laid a foundation, and someone else is building upon it. Let each one take care how he builds upon it. For no one can lay a foundation other than that which is laid, which is Jesus Christ. Now if anyone builds on the foundation with gold, silver, precious stones, wood, hay, straw—each one's work will become manifest, for the Day will disclose it, because it will be revealed by fire, and the fire will test what sort of work each one has done. If the work that anyone has built on the foundation survives, he will receive a reward. If anyone's work is burned up, he will suffer loss, though he himself will be saved, but only as through fire. (1 Cor. 3:10–15)

So the prospect of heavenly rewards is a legitimate motivation for good works in this life. However, we must keep certain facts in mind.

First, if we do things in this world strictly to try to get rewards in heaven, we will get nothing. The rewards will be given to the humble servant who does not seek them. These rewards involve God's crowning His own gifts. The rewards are gracious rewards.

Second, once we are in heaven, we will agree with God's decisions concerning who got what rewards, and we will be fully satisfied with our positions for eternity.

The following passages have more to say about rewards in heaven and punishments in hell:

"Therefore whoever relaxes one of the least of these commandments and teaches others to do the same will be called least in the kingdom of heaven, but whoever does them and teaches them will be called great in the kingdom of heaven." (Matt. 5:19)

"Do not lay up for yourselves treasures on earth, where moth and rust destroy and where thieves break in and steal, but lay up for yourselves treasures in heaven, where neither moth nor rust destroys and where thieves do not break in and steal. For where your treasure is, there your heart will be also." (Matt. 6:19–21)

"But I tell you, it will be more bearable on the day of judgment for Tyre and Sidon than for you. And you, Capernaum, will you be exalted to heaven? You will be brought down to Hades. If the miracles done in you had been done in Sodom, it would have remained until this day. But I tell you that it will be more tolerable on the day of judgment for the land of Sodom than for you." (Matt. 11:22–24)

"Woe to you, scribes and Pharisees, hypocrites! For you devour widows' houses and for a pretense you make long prayers; therefore you will receive the greater condemnation." (Matt. 23:14)

"And he who had received the five talents came forward, bringing five talents more, saying, 'Master, you delivered to me five talents; here I have made five talents more.' His master said to him, 'Well done, good and faithful servant. You have been faithful over a little; I will set you over much. Enter into the joy of your master.' . . . For to everyone who has will more be given, and he will have an abundance. But from the one who has not, even what he has will be taken away. And cast the worthless servant into the outer darkness. In that place there will be weeping and gnashing of teeth." (Matt. 25:20–21, 29–30)

"And that servant who knew his master's will but did not get ready or act according to his will, will receive a severe beating. But the one who did not know, and did what deserved a beating, will receive a light beating. Everyone to whom much was given, of him much will be required, and from him to whom they entrusted much, they will demand the more." (Luke 12:47–48)

Jesus answered him, "You would have no authority over me at all unless it had been given you from above. Therefore he who delivered me over to you has the greater sin." (John 19:11)

Clearly Scripture summons us to do good works. It shows us that God commands good works. It reveals that we should live obedient lives out of thankfulness. And it holds out the prospect of rewards in heaven as a result of good works in this life. Even though our deeds contribute nothing to our salvation, we still have abundant motivation to do good.

NOTES

1   R.C. Sproul, *Now, That's a Good Question!* (Wheaton, Ill.: Tyndale House, 1996), 287.

2   William Hendriksen, *The Bible on the Life Hereafter* (Grand Rapids, Mich.: Baker Books, 1959), 93.

Chapter 5

Dilemma Three—
obedience

If God has predetermined everything
that comes to pass, why should we spend
valuable time in prayer or evangelism?

C alvinism has been criticized for
putting a lack of emphasis on
prayer and evangelism. In fact, because the Reformed faith
emphasizes God's sovereignty by proclaiming that He has
determined everything that will happen and who will be
saved, some say Calvinism makes praying and evangelizing
pointless.

This criticism is based on a misunderstanding. The
truth is that Calvinism teaches that prayer and evangelism

are crucial aspects of the Christian life, and that there are numerous good reasons to do both. Let's begin by considering prayer.

John Calvin, the man for whom the doctrinal system known as "Calvinism" was named, saw great value in prayer. In fact, he devoted seventy pages to this subject in his book, *Institutes of the Christian Religion.* He wrote, "To know God as the master and bestower of all good things, who invites us to request them of him, and still not go to him and not ask of him—this would be of as little profit as for a man to neglect a treasure, buried and hidden in the earth, after it had been pointed out to him."[1]

Still, the question remains: Since God has predetermined everything, why pray? I believe Scripture gives us at least six great reasons to pray.

First, God commands it. Is this not reason enough to do anything in this life? In the following verses, God gives us great motivation for prayer and encourages us to come to Him with our problems and desires:

> *[Pray] at all times in the Spirit, with all prayer and supplication. To that end keep alert with all perseverance, making supplication for all the saints, and also for me, that words may be given to me in opening my mouth boldly to proclaim the mystery of the gospel. (Eph. 6:18–19)*

Do not be anxious about anything, but in everything by prayer and supplication with thanksgiving let your requests be made known to God. (Phil. 4:6)

Is anyone among you suffering? Let him pray. (James 5:13a)

Second, prayer is a means of worshiping God. Any time we do what God desires, we are honoring Him. By coming to God in prayer, we obey His command, thereby showing that He is our Lord. Praying on our knees is one way to worship Him and show our submission to Him.

Be still before the LORD and wait patiently for him. (Ps. 37:7a)

Praise is due you, O God, in Zion, to you shall vows be performed. O you who hears prayer, to you shall all flesh come. (Ps. 65:1–2)

The LORD is far from the wicked, but he hears the prayer of the righteous. (Prov. 15:29)

Pray without ceasing, give thanks in all circumstances; for this is the will of God in Christ Jesus for you. (1 Thess. 5:17–18)

Third, prayer is a blessing to us. We come away from prayer refreshed with the knowledge that we have met with the almighty God:

The LORD is near to all who call on him, to all who call on him in truth. (Ps. 145:18)

Draw near to God, and he will draw near to you. (James 4:8a)

We have confidence before God; and whatever we ask we receive from him, because we keep his commandments and do what pleases him. (1 John 3:21b–22)

Fourth, prayer helps us see our insufficiency. We learn that we are not independent of God. Prayer shows us that we need Him:

"Your Father knows what you need before you ask him." (Matt. 6:8b)

The Spirit helps us in our weakness. For we do not know what to pray for as we ought, but the Spirit himself intercedes for us with groanings too deep for words. (Rom. 8:26)

Fifth, God uses prayer to bring about His predetermined will. Prayer does not change God's mind. God not only ordains ends, He ordains the means that He uses to bring about those ends.

In the story of Elijah and the prophets of Baal, Elijah was sure of God's purpose and promised rain to King Ahab. However, he still prayed anxiously with his head between his knees. He had no fear that his prophecy would be discredited, but he knew it was his duty to lay his desires before God:

So Ahab went up to eat and to drink. And Elijah went up to the top of Mount Carmel. And he bowed himself down on the earth and put his face between his knees. (1 Kings 18:42)

This is the confidence that we have toward him, that if we ask anything according to his will he hears us. (1 John 5:14)

Sixth, prayer teaches us to depend upon God and His sovereignty rather than ourselves. Prayer can be a daily reminder that we are not in control, but rather in the arms of a loving heavenly Father:

Consider my affliction and my trouble, and forgive all my sins. (Ps. 25:18)

Call upon me in the day of trouble; I will deliver you, and you shall glorify me. (Ps. 50:15)

Hear my cry, O God, listen to my prayer; from the end of the earth I call to you when my heart is faint. Lead me to the rock that is higher than I. (Ps. 61:1–2)

Then I turned my face to the Lord God, seeking him by prayer and pleas for mercy with fasting and sackcloth and ashes. (Dan. 9:3)

And when he had entered the house, his disciples asked him privately, "Why could we not cast it out?" And he said to them, "This kind cannot be driven out by anything but prayer." (Mark 9:28–29)

If we confess our sins, he is faithful and just to forgive us our sins and cleanse us from all unrighteousness. (1 John 1:9)

The Bible gives us many great examples of prayer, but we will look briefly at two. First, there is the Lord's Prayer, which teaches us to pray "'your will be done, on earth as it is in heaven'" (Matt. 6:10). We are instructed here to pray as if we understand that God reigns in this world. By doing so, we are agreeing with the Calvinistic doctrine that God's will is supreme. But we are still praying. God uses our prayers to bring about those things He already has determined. How can that be? Is not God so much greater than we ever imagined?

The second great prayer in the Bible is in Acts 4:24–30. In verses 27–28, the disciples said that God "anointed" Herod and Pontius Pilate "'to do whatever your hand and your plan had predestined to take place.'" Then, in verse 29, they concluded by saying, "'And now, Lord, look upon their threats and grant to your servants to continue to speak your word with all boldness.'" Those who were praying here said they knew things were happening the way God had planned them, but they still prayed that He would work in them. They knew that prayer mattered.

We cannot understand this; it is a mystery, just like the issue of God's sovereignty and man's responsibility that we discussed in Chapter 3. But the fact that we cannot understand how God can predetermine everything, yet our prayers still matter and are heard, does not mean both facts are not true.

In an article titled "The Prayers of the Righteous Are Never Futile," R. C. Sproul wrote:

If God is sovereign, why pray? When I pray to God I am talking to One who has all knowledge. One who cannot possibly learn anything from me that He doesn't already know. He knows everything there is to know, including what's on my mind. He knows what I'm going to say to Him before I say it. He knows what He's going to do before He does it. His knowledge is sovereign, as He is sovereign.

People may ask: "Does prayer change God's mind?" To ask such a question is to answer it. What kind of God could be influenced by my prayers? What could my prayers do to induce Him to change His plans? Could I possibly give God any information about anything that He doesn't already have? Or could I persuade Him toward a more excellent way by my superior wisdom? Of course not. I am completely unqualified to be God's mentor or His guidance counselor. So the simple answer is that prayer does not change God's mind.

"Does prayer change things?" Now, the answer is an emphatic Yes! The Scriptures tell us that "the effective fervent prayer of a righteous man avails much" (James 5:16). What then does prayer change? In the first place, my prayers change me. My time with God is for my edification, not His. Prayer also changes things. In practical terms, we say that prayer works. Prayer is one of the means God uses to bring about the ends He ordains.[2]

We pray expectantly and confidently, not in spite of the sovereignty of God, but because of it. Note these verses:

"Therefore I tell you, whatever you ask in prayer, believe that you have received it, and it will be yours." (Mark 11:24)

That person must not suppose that he will receive anything from the Lord; he is a double-minded man, unstable in all his ways. (James 1:7–8)

Calvin says about these verses, "It is amazing how much our lack of trust provokes God if we request of him a boon that we do not expect."[3]

Now let us turn our attention to evangelism. Just as God does not need our prayers, He does not need us to bring about the salvation of His people. However, He commands that we participate in evangelism and He uses ordinary people like us to accomplish His plan. God is the primary or first cause of everything that happens in the universe. We, however, are the secondary cause, the means God uses to bring about His will.

Scripture is very clear about our role in reaching unbelievers. The words of Jesus in Matthew 28:18–20, a passage known as the Great Commission, are especially pointed:

"All authority in heaven and on earth has been given to me. Go therefore and make disciples of all nations, baptizing them in the name of the Father and of the Son and of the Holy Spirit, teaching them to observe all that I have commanded you. And behold, I am with you always, to the end of the age."

Other verses are no less clear:

"He commanded us to preach to the people and to testify that he is the one appointed by God to be judge of the living and the dead." (Acts 10:42)

"You will be a witness for him to everyone of what you have seen and heard." (Acts 22:15)

Preach the word; be ready in season and out of season; reprove, rebuke, and exhort, with complete patience and teaching. (2 Tim. 4:2)

In your hearts regard Christ the Lord as holy, always being prepared to make a defense to anyone who asks you for a reason for the hope that is in you. (1 Peter 3:15a)

How are they to call on him in whom they have not believed? And how are they to believe in him of whom they have never heard? And how are they to hear without someone preaching? And how are they to preach unless they are sent? As it is written, 'How beautiful are the feet of those who preach the good news. (Rom. 10:14–15)

This last verse sums it up well. It is a great privilege to be used by God as a secondary cause to bring someone to faith in Him. Jonah was basically a reluctant secondary cause, but God changed his heart and used him to bring salvation to the city of Nineveh. God is always the initiator; He alone can work in someone's heart. But we are the means He uses to bring about that end. That truly is good news.

Have you ever been in a situation when you were presenting the gospel to someone and the correct words flowed out of your mouth even though you were not sure where they came from? Maybe you were able to remember verses that you normally forget or quote a book or sermon that you had read or heard years earlier. God promises to fill our minds with the truth when we are active in spreading His Word.

What about the person who wants Jesus but isn't wanted by Him? Here is the simple answer: *There is no such person!* Consider the testimony of Scripture:

> *"You will seek me and find me. When you seek me with all of your heart, I will be found by you, declares the LORD."* (Jer. 29:13–14a)

> *"Ask, and it will be given to you; seek, and you will find; knock, and it will be opened to you. For everyone who asks receives, and the one who seeks finds, and to the one who knocks it will be opened." (Matt. 7:7–8)*

> *"All that the Father gives me will come to me, and whoever comes to me I will never cast out." (John 6:37)*

There has never been a person who wanted to be a Christian to whom God said no. The Reformed faith holds that when a person wants to be a Christian, God already has worked in his heart, and Scripture assures us that "he who began a good work in you will bring it to completion" (Phil 1:6).

The Reformed faith also eliminates the "worry" aspect of

evangelism. Have you ever heard someone say that he is to blame for another person not becoming a Christian because he never talked to that person about Christ or shared the gospel with him or her? God commands us to always be "prepared to make a defense to anyone who asks you for a reason for the hope that is in you" (1 Peter 3:15b), but we do not have to live in fear that a friend or relative will go to hell if we do not do so. If someone is elect, God will find a willing secondary cause to bring that person to Himself. Neither should we worry if we only introduce the gospel to a friend who then moves away. Again, God's promise to complete the good work He begins provides comfort. If God uses a believer to plant a seed, He can bring another to water it.

Calvinists, then, are as fully committed to prayer and evangelism as any other Christians. Believing in the sovereignty of God and in His choice to use human beings to carry out His will, Calvinists fall to their knees in prayer and rise up to share the glorious gospel of Jesus Christ.

NOTES

1   John Calvin, *Institutes of the Christian Religion* (Philadelphia, Pa.: Westminster Press, 1960), 850.

2   R. C. Sproul, "The Prayers of the Righteous Are Never Futile," *byFaith* magazine (January/February 2005), 21.

3   Calvin, *Institutes of the Christian Religion*, 863.

Chapter 6

Dilemma Four—Evil

Since God created everything and He cannot sin, how did evil come into being?

O f all the topics covered in this book, the question of evil is probably the most difficult. One major reason is that the origin of evil is not firmly established in the Scriptures. There is a great mystery here.

That fact leaves us with many tough questions: Does God's providence cover all events that occur in history or only the "good" ones? Does anything occur in this world outside of God's sovereign control? Does Satan have a free reign in this world or are his actions within the sovereignty of God?

As we begin to think through these questions, let's consider three events from modern history:

- The tsunami that killed more than two hundred thousand people around the Indian Ocean in December 2004.
- The devastating terrorist attacks on the United States on Sept. 11, 2001.
- The holocaust in Germany during World War II.

Were these events within God's providence or outside of it? Those are the only logical options, as these diagrams demonstrate:

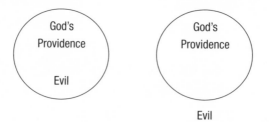

When we listen to the popular media, it is not unusual to hear it said that a good God could not have had anything to do with events such as the tsunami, the attacks of 9/11, or the Holocaust. This is not surprising. These events seem to call God's goodness into question, and some who call themselves believers wish to prevent unbelievers from casting accusations against Him. So they attempt to remove responsibility from God.

But if we say that God's providence does not extend over evil, we are making a strong statement about God. If evil things can happen over which God has no control, what is He like? Thinking this way limits the power of God by casting Him as a being who is at the mercy of His own creation.

When we turn to Scripture, however, we find a very different picture. The Bible tells us that God not only permits evil, He even ordains it:

> *Then the Lord said to him, "Who has made man's mouth? Who makes him mute, or deaf, or seeing, or blind? Is it not I, the Lord?" (Ex. 4:11)*

> *"Shall we receive good from God, and shall we not receive evil?" In all this Job did not sin with his lips. (Job 2:10b)*

> *"I form light and create darkness, I make well-being and create calamity, I am the Lord, who does all these things." (Isa. 45:7)*

> *Who has spoken and it came to pass, unless the Lord has commanded it? Is it not from the mouth of the Most High that good and bad come? (Lam. 3:37–38)*

"Is a trumpet blown in a city, and the people are not afraid? Does disaster come to a city, unless the LORD has done it?" (Amos 3:6)

These verses say that God causes deafness, muteness, and blindness; that He decrees calamities; that trouble comes from Him; and that He causes disasters.

Clearly, *nothing* is outside the providence of God, and that includes evil. Everything that happens in this world comes from the hand of God. That means Satan does not have a free reign—he can act only within the limits of God's permission. God is not powerless over Satan and evil.

The great news for Christians is found in Romans 8:28: "And we know that for those who love God all things work together for good, for those who are called according to his purpose!"

What is this "good" that the Scriptures mention? Is it our happiness, our financial security, or our success in this life? No, it is none of these. The good that God promises is our ultimate good—the opportunity to live in the new heavens and the new earth with Him for eternity.

Paul wrote in Philippians 1:21–24: "For to me to live is Christ, and to die is gain. If I am to live in the flesh, that means fruitful labor for me. . . . I am hard pressed between the two. My desire is to depart and be with Christ, for that is far better. But to remain in the flesh is more necessary on your account." Paul knew the ultimate "good" that is promised to believers, and because of that he could praise God in any circumstance, good or evil, that befell him.

Paul added in 2 Corinthians 4:17–18: "For this slight momentary affliction is preparing for us an eternal weight of glory beyond all comparison, as we look not to the things that are seen but to the things that are unseen. For the things that are seen are transient, but the things that are unseen are eternal."

Although God decrees evil, He does not directly perform morally evil deeds. God cannot do moral evil because His will is directed only toward good. However, God allows Satan, demons, and sinful men to do evil deeds. He does not *cause* them to do anything they don't want to do; He merely *allows* them to carry out their evil intentions. Thus, man is responsible for his sin, not God.

As James wrote: "Let no one say when he is tempted, 'I am being tempted by God,' for God cannot be tempted with evil, and he himself tempts no one. But each person is tempted when he is lured and enticed by his own desire. Then desire when it has conceived gives birth to sin, and sin when it is fully grown brings forth death" (James 1:13–15).

What is the most evil and terrible event that has ever

occurred? All Christians agree that it was the death of Christ—and the Scriptures make clear that God ordained that event:

> *"Men of Israel, hear these words: Jesus of Nazareth, a man attested to you by God with mighty works and wonders and signs that God did through him in your midst, as you yourselves know—this Jesus, delivered up according to the definite plan and foreknowledge of God, you crucified and killed by the hands of lawless men." (Acts 2:22–23)*

> *"For truly in this city there were gathered together against your holy servant Jesus, whom you anointed, both Herod and Pontius Pilate, along with the Gentiles and the peoples of Israel, to do whatever your hand and your plan had predestined to take place." (Acts 4:27–28)*

God knew that Jesus would be put to death on the cross, for God had designed the atonement. It was His plan that Jesus would die, but evil men actually caused Jesus' death. God ordained the events of Jesus' crucifixion, but man was responsible for the evil that occurred. God did not betray Jesus; Judas did. God did not sentence Jesus to crucifixion; Pilate did. God did not nail Jesus to the cross; the soldiers did.

When Christ died, Satan must have been thinking that he had finally gotten rid of the Son of God. Perhaps he believed he had shown that he was greater than God, for he apparently had spoiled God's plan by killing His Son. But as the Scriptures reveal, God was able to bring "ultimate" good out of that evil event:

> *For Christ also suffered once for sins, the righteous for the unrighteous, that he might bring us to God, being put to death in the flesh but made alive in the spirit. (1 Peter 3:18)*

God's objective is to bring His elect to Himself. If an "evil" event causes that result, whether it is the death of His Son or a natural disaster, we can only rejoice in the end result that He so graciously accomplishes.

One of the best scriptural illustration of these truths is the story of Joseph and his brothers, found in Genesis 37–50. It is probably the strongest biblical example of the concurrence of the will of God and the will of the creature.

This story is filled with evil events. The first was the sale of Joseph into slavery. This evil was committed by his brothers, but it fulfilled God's purpose to send Joseph to Egypt. The next evil was the false accusation of Joseph by Potiphar's wife, but that fulfilled God's purpose of sending Joseph to prison so he could meet Pharaoh's servants and eventually bring about the salvation of His people. Understanding these things, Joseph could tell his brothers years later, "'You meant evil against me, but God meant it for good, to bring it about that many people should be kept alive, as they are today'" (Gen. 50:20b).

We cannot see God's purposes. Sometimes He lets us in on a piece or two. But when we see only a part, a particular event may not make sense or we may think that God has made a mistake. God, however, does not make mistakes. Every event that has ever occurred in the history of the world was under His providential control.

The story of Lazarus is an excellent example. Jesus was not late arriving at the home of Mary and Martha. He did not make a mistake in coming after the death of His friend, Lazarus, forcing Him to perform a miracle to make up for His indiscretion. Jesus clearly stated in John 11:4: "'This illness does not lead to death. It is for the glory of God, so that the Son of God may be glorified through it.'" Jesus allowed His friend to die so that a greater good could be accomplished from it. That is how we need to look at the existence of evil.

There are two big questions with which philosophers have struggled in regard to the existence of evil. The first is "Does the existence of evil prove God does not exist or is not all-powerful?" The second is the "why" question: "Why does evil exist?"

Does the fact that evil exists in itself prove that God does not exist or that He is not all-powerful? A secular philosopher could reason as follows:

A wholly good being eliminates all the evil that it can. ↪

If God exists, God is wholly good. ↪

If God exists, He eliminates all the evil that He can. ↪

An omnipotent being can eliminate all evil. ↪

If God exists, God is omnipotent. ↪

If God exists, God can eliminate all evil. ↪

If God exists, God eliminates all evil. ↪

If God exists, there is no evil. ↪

There is evil. ↪

God does not exist.

There are two fundamental problems with the secular philosopher's line of reasoning. First, there is no reason to start this process with the belief that God, as a wholly good being, would eliminate all the evil that He can. Stating this eliminates the possibility that good can come out of evil events that God controls. The foremost such event was Christ's death on the cross, but Romans 8:28 assures us that *all* things work for the good of believers—the ultimate good of getting to heaven and living with God for eternity. We would not want God to eliminate events that might move us closer to this blessed future.

The second fact that destroys this syllogism is that God *does* exist. The fact that He has shown Himself, not only in nature but through His personal intervention in this world, not only leaves man without excuse (Rom. 1:20) but destroys this argument by the secular philosopher.

This brings us to the more difficult question, the "why" question. Why does evil exist at all? In other words, if God is good and He created everything, how did evil come into the world?

We do not know the answer to this question. The Bible is silent. R. C. Sproul says this will be the first question he will ask once he gets to heaven.

I'm going to go out on a limb and give you my educated theory as to why evil exists. I call it my "Theory of Opposites."

Everything in this world has an opposite:

> white — black
> fast — slow
> light — dark
> smart — dumb
> reading this book — not reading this book
> me (fill in your name) — not me (fill in someone else's name)

For everything you can possibly think of there is an opposite. In many instances, the opposite is just the nonexistence of the item in question. For example, football—no football or food—no food.

Opposites are very important. To understand something, you must know its opposite. What would white be if we did not know about black? How could we define smart if we did not understand dumbness? How could we recognize that something is fast if we did not comprehend slowness?

I believe this is why evil exists. God created everything good. He did not create anything evil. But when He created good, evil automatically came into being as the antithesis or opposite of good. We could not really understand or comprehend "good" if we did not know "evil."

Listen to Paul's amazing thoughts on this subject:

What then shall we say? That the law is sin? By no means! Yet if it had not been for the law, I would not have known sin. I would not have known what it is to covet if the law had not said, "You shall not covet." But sin, seizing an opportunity through the commandment, produced in me all kinds of covetousness. Apart from the law, sin lies dead. I was once alive apart from the law, but when the commandment came, sin came alive and I died. The very commandment that promised life proved to be death to me. For sin, seizing an opportunity through

the commandment, deceived me and through it killed me.
So the law is holy, and the commandment is holy and
righteous and good. Did that which is good, then, bring
death to me? By no means! It was sin, producing death
in me through what is good, in order that sin might be
shown to be sin. (Rom. 7:7–13a)

Paul says here that God's good gift of the law to the
human race had the effect of producing sin and death. But
these negative effects also revealed the sin that was present in the human heart, that a solution might be sought
through God's redeeming grace. The good revealed the
evil, and vice versa.

Sproul touched on this philosophy in his January 2007
Message of the Month lecture:

Evil is always explained or described in negative
terms. Evil is a parasite insofar as the parasite depends upon its host for its own existence. Once the
host dies, the parasite perishes as well, because the
parasite cannot live independently from the host.
In that sense, evil is parasitical. It depends on the
good for its very definition.

We talk about evil in terms of *un*righteousness,
*im*perfection, law*less*ness, and *dis*obedience, so that
we understand evil only against the background of the

prior standard of goodness. Evil is only known insofar as it fails to conform to the standard of goodness.

The very presence of evil bears witness to the prior existence of the good![1]

The great church father Augustine expressed this same theory in his book *Soliloquies*. According to historical theologian Thomas J. Nettles, Augustine argued:

Since God created everything, evil does not have an existence independent of good things. Evil is a privation of good. When all good is gone, nothing exists. Evil is only an absence of good. It is not an independent substance that invades and contaminates, but must borrow from God's good and diminish its glory. The substances in which evil resides are themselves good. Evil is removed not by eradication of a contrary nature . . . but by purifying of the thing itself which was thus depraved. Truth and falsehood dwell in the same tension, according to Augustine, for nothing is false except by some imitation of the true.[2]

This "Theory of Opposites" clears God of creating evil, but allows it to exist in the world and be used by God for His divine purposes.

NOTES

1   R. C. Sproul, "The Problem of Evil," *Message of the Month* CD (Lake Mary, Fla.: Ligonier Ministries, January 2007).

2   Thomas J. Nettles, "Augustine, Doctor of Grace," *Tabletalk* magazine (August 2005), 10.

Chapter 7

Dilemma Five— Babies

If people are born totally depraved, as Calvinism says, where do babies go when they die?

S ometime in your life you will know someone, Christian or non-Christian, who had a miscarriage, suffered the death of an infant, or chose to have an abortion. What will you tell that person when he or she asks you where that baby is spending eternity? What will be the basis for your answer?

There are five possibilities for what happens to babies who die:

- They all go to hell. If a person must make a decision to believe in Christ in order to get to heaven, all babies who die must be condemned, since babies cannot make a decision to believe in Christ.

- Only those who are baptized go to heaven. This is basically the Roman Catholic view. Catholics believe that baptism is necessary for salvation and that it guarantees salvation. That is why it is so important for a Catholic baby who is sick to be given the sacrament of baptism.

- Only covenant babies (children of believers) go to heaven. This is a belief based on the promise God gave when He made a covenant with Abraham: "'I will establish my covenant between me and you and your offspring after you'" (Gen. 17:7a).

- Only those who are elect go to heaven. Those who are not elect go to hell. We have no idea who the elect babies are, any more than we know who the elect adults are.

- They all go to heaven. Because of special grace of God, all babies who die, whether born of Christian or non-Christian parents, get to heaven. This is another way of saying that all babies who die are elect.

There are Christians who hold to each of these views. There is human logic behind each of them. However, I agree with the fifth view. I am positive that all elect babies who die go to heaven. I have confidence that all babies of Christian parents are elect. And I believe and trust that God saves all babies who die by His perfect grace. I will spend the rest of this chapter trying to convince you of my conclusions.

We must admit from the outset that babies are not free from the curse of original sin. All children are conceived as sinners and are born morally corrupt, not good or neutral. They may be innocent of personal sin, but they are not innocent of the imputed sin of Adam, just as Scripture teaches:

> *"I will never again curse the ground because of man, for the intention of man's heart is evil from his youth." (Gen. 8:21b)*

> *Behold, I was brought forth in iniquity, and in sin did my mother conceive me. (Ps. 51:5)*

> *The wicked are estranged from the womb; they go astray from birth, speaking lies. (Ps. 58:3)*

> *Enter not into judgment with your servant, for no one living is righteous before you. (Ps. 143:2)*

> *Surely there is not a righteous man on earth who does good and never sins. (Eccl. 7:20)*

> *"None is righteous; no, not one." (Rom. 3:10)*

Among whom we all once lived in the passions of our flesh, carrying out the desires of the body and the mind, and were by nature children of wrath, like the rest of mankind. (Eph. 2:3)

Since all babies are born depraved, it would be logical to assume that all babies who die go to hell. After all, they cannot repent or believe in Jesus. As Calvinists, shouldn't we believe that *no* babies are elect, since God obviously did not choose them to live and become Christians?

Reformed theology holds that this statement is not correct.

Charles H. Spurgeon, the great Reformed Baptist preacher of nineteenth century London, stated it this way:

Among the gross falsehoods which have been uttered against the Calvinists proper is the wicked calumny that we hold the damnation of little infants. But a baser lie was never uttered. There may have existed somewhere in some corner of the earth a miscreant (criminal) who would dare to say that there were infants in hell but I have never met with him nor have I met with a man who ever saw such a person. We say with regard to infants, Scripture saith but little, and therefore where Scripture is confessedly scant it is for no man to determine dogmatically, but I think I speak for the entire body or certainly with exceedingly few exceptions, and those unknown to me, when I say we hold that all infants who die are elect of God and are therefore saved, and we look to this as being the means by which Christ shall see of the travail of his soul to a great degree, and we do sometimes hope that thus the multitude of the saved shall be made to exceed the multitude of the lost. Whatever view our friends may hold upon the point, they are not necessarily connected with Calvinistic doctrine. I believe that the Lord Jesus who said that such is the kingdom of heaven doth daily and constantly receive into his loving arms those tender ones who were only shown and then snatched away to heaven.[1]

Likewise, B. B. Warfield, the great Princeton theologian, explained God's relationship to infants in this manner:

The destiny of infants who die is determined irrespective of their choice by an unconditional decree of God suspended for its execution on no act of their own. Their salvation is wrought by an unconditional application of the grace of Christ to their souls through the immediate and irresistible cooperation of the Holy Spirit prior to and apart from any action of their own proper wills. If death in infancy does depend on God's providence, it is assuredly God in His providence who selects this vast multitude to be made participants of His own conditional salvation. This is but to say that they are unconditionally predestined to salvation from the foundation of the world. If only a single infant dying in irresponsible infancy be saved the whole Arminian principle is traversed. If all infants who die in such are saved, not only the majority of the saved but that majority of the human race hitherto have entered into life by a non-Arminian pathway.[2]

Contemporary Presbyterian theologian R.C. Sproul says the following on this issue:

We hope and have a certain level of confidence that God will be particularly gracious toward those who have never had the opportunity to be exposed to the gospel, such as infants and children who are too disabled to hear and understand. The New Testament does not teach us this explicitly. It does tell us a lot about the character of God—about

His mercy and grace—and gives us every reason to have that kind of confidence in His dealings with children.[3]

Reformed theology holds that we are saved exclusively by grace. Fallen, sinful, guilty, depraved children who die have no merit of their own. Like adults, they must be saved by grace. Christ bore the sins for all those who could believe *and* for all who could not. The fact that infants are too young to respond to that grace with faith is immaterial. Grace is based on no merit of any kind within the sinner. Salvation is based on sovereign choice for adults as well as infants. All are saved by grace. In the Arminian system, such assurance about dying infants is impossible. Arminians believe man has to contribute to his salvation by exercising saving faith. Thus, only Reformed theology makes it possible to comfort a grieving mother at the death of her infant.

As both Spurgeon and Sproul note in their comments above, there is no explicit teaching on the eternal destination of dying babies. But Scripture nevertheless gives us much reason to hope that they are saved. One strong Scriptural support for the salvation of dying infants is God's attitude toward children. Clearly He has a special care for them:

You are he who took me from the womb; you made me trust you at my mother's breasts. On you was I cast from my birth, and from my mother's womb you have been my God. (Ps. 22:9–10)

"Before I formed you in the womb I knew you, and before you were born I consecrated you." (Jer. 1:5a)

And when Elizabeth heard the greeting of Mary, the baby leaped in her womb. And Elizabeth was filled with the Holy Spirit. (Luke 1:41)

He . . . had set me apart before I was born, and . . . called me by his grace. (Gal. 1:15)

These verses prove that God has a great love for little ones. He knows them, He cares about them, and He is committed to saving them.

The very best example of this divine love for children may be Psalm 139: 1–17:

O LORD, you have searched me and known me! You know when I sit down and when I rise up; you discern my thoughts from afar. You search out my path and my lying down and are acquainted with all my ways. Even before a word is on my tongue, behold, O LORD, you know it altogether. You hem me in, behind and before, and lay your hand upon me. Such knowledge is too wonderful for me; it is high; I cannot attain it. Where shall I go from your Spirit? Or where shall I flee from your presence? If I ascend to heaven, you are there! If I make my bed in Sheol, you are there! If I take the wings of the morning and dwell in the uttermost parts of the sea, even there your hand shall lead me, and your right hand shall hold me. If I say "Surely the darkness shall cover me, and the light about me be night," even the darkness is not dark to you; the night is bright as day, for darkness is as light with you. For you formed my inward parts; you knitted me together in my mother's womb. I praise you, for I am fearfully and wonderfully made. Wonderful are your works; my soul knows it very well. My frame was not hidden from you, when I was being made in secret, intricately woven in the depths of the earth. Your eyes saw my unformed substance; in your book were written, every one of them, the days that were formed for me, when as yet there were none of them. How precious to me are your thoughts, O God! How vast is the sum of them!

In that final sentence, David affirmed that his earlier statements were a treasured truth. The fact that God knew him before the world was created and while he was in his mother's womb was wonderful to consider.

During the time of His incarnation, Jesus exhibited this same care for little ones: "Jesus said, 'Let the little children come to me and do not hinder them, for to such belongs the kingdom of heaven.' And he laid his hands on them and went away" (Matt. 19:14–15). Placing hands on the children was Jesus' way of giving them His blessing. Clearly He felt a special care for them.

The best indication that God saves infants who die is found in 2 Samuel 12:15b–23, which records the sad outcome of the story of David's sin with Bathsheba:

And the LORD afflicted the child that Uriah's wife bore to David, and he became sick. David therefore sought God on behalf of the child. And David fasted and went in and lay all night on the ground. And the elders of his house stood beside him, to raise him from the ground, but he would not, nor did he eat food with them. On the seventh day the child died. And the servants of David were afraid to tell him that the child was dead, for they said, "Behold, while the child was yet alive, we spoke to him, and he did not listen to us. How then can we say to him the child is dead? He may do himself some harm." But when David saw that his servants were whispering together, David understood that the child was dead. And David said to his servants, "Is the child dead?" They said, "He is dead." Then David arose from the earth and washed and anointed himself and changed his clothes. And he went into the house of the LORD and worshiped. He then went to his own house. And when he asked, they set food before him, and he ate. Then his servants said to him, "What is this thing that you have done? You fasted and wept for the child while he was alive; but when the child died, you arose and ate food." He said, "While the child was still alive, I fasted and wept, for I said, 'Who knows whether the LORD will be gracious to me, that the child may live.' But now he is dead. Why should I fast? Can I bring him back again? I shall go to him, but he will not return to me."

Hope replaced sorrow in David's heart. He knew where he was going when he left this earth. In Psalm 23:6, David declared, "Surely goodness and mercy shall follow me all the days of my life, and I shall dwell in the house of the LORD forever." And just as David knew he would be taken to heaven someday, he knew he would see his son there. He had total confidence that this infant who had died was with God.

David had other sons, one of whom was Absalom, who led a rebellion against his father and God. When Absalom finally fell in battle and David received the news, he reacted in a very different manner: "And the king was deeply moved and went up to the chamber over the gate and wept. And as he went, he said, 'O my son Absalom, my son, my son Absalom! Would I had died instead of you, O Absalom, my son, my son!'" (2 Sam. 18:33).

The king was deeply moved and he wept. This was the opposite of what had happened when the baby died. David knew that Absalom was not in heaven, so he had great sorrow. He would have preferred to have died himself so that Absalom could keep living, since life on this earth was all that Absalom had.

Another interesting Old Testament story concerns Jeroboam, a wicked king of Israel who worshiped other gods. He also had a son, Abijah, who became very ill. At that time, God said:

> *"Thus says the LORD, the God of Israel: . . . 'Behold, I will bring harm upon the house of Jeroboam and will cut off from Jeroboam every male, both bond and free in Israel, and will burn up the house of Jeroboam, as a man burns up dung until it is all gone. Anyone belonging to Jeroboam who dies in the city the dogs shall eat, and anyone who dies in the open country the birds of the heavens shall eat, for the LORD has spoken it.' Arise therefore, go to your house. When your feet enter the city, the child shall die.*

And all Israel shall mourn for him and bury him, for he only of Jeroboam shall come to the grave, because in him there is found something pleasing to the LORD, the God of Israel, in the house of Jeroboam." (1 Kings 14:7–13)

The baby was saved, but the rest of the entire household was damned. God found something "good" in an infant of non-believing parents.

Here are some other scriptural reasons I believe we can confidently assert that all babies who die go to heaven:

First, have you ever heard someone say, "I wish I had never been born"? Well, characters in the Bible express that very thought from time to time:

"Why did I not die at birth, come out from the womb and expire?" (Job 3:11)

"Or why was I not as a hidden stillborn child, as infants who never see the light?" (Job 3:16)

If a man fathers a hundred children and lives many years, so that the days of his years are many, but his soul is not satisfied with life's good things, and he also has no burial, I say that a stillborn child is better off than he. (Eccl. 6:3)

Have you ever wondered about these verses? Why did these men say it is better to die in infancy? Could it be because all babies go to heaven, and these men knew that if they had died as infants, they would have gone directly there? I believe they did. They were rightly expressing a desire to have been with God rather than to have lived the life they did on this earth.

Second, Scripture records two mass murders of infants. In Exodus 1:22, we read, "Then Pharaoh commanded all his people, 'Every son that is born to the Hebrews you shall cast into the Nile, but you shall let every daughter live.'" And Matthew 2:16–18 says: "Then Herod, when he saw that he had been tricked by the wise men, became furious, and he sent and killed all the male children in Bethlehem and in all that region who were two years old or under, according to the time that he had ascertained from the wise men. Then was fulfilled what was spoken by the prophet Jeremiah: 'A voice was heard in Ramah, weeping and loud lamentation, Rachel weeping for her children; she refused to be comforted, because they are no more.'"

How could a loving God allow these children to be murdered in this manner? Moses was saved by Pharaoh's daughter and Jesus escaped with His parents to Egypt, but what about all those babies who died? These were Jewish infants, Abraham's seed. How could God do this?

If we look at these two scenarios with the understanding that all those infants went to heaven and got to be with

God immediately, rather than having to live their difficult lives first, we see that they were greatly blessed.

Third, hell is always described by a list of abominations that a person commits. In His grace, God takes some infants before they can develop such a list: "And the dead were judged by what was written in the books, according to what they had done" (Rev. 20:12b). Men are saved by grace, but they are damned by works. What works have babies done?

In John 8:24, Jesus says, "'I told you that you would die in your sins, for unless you believe that I am he you will die in your sins.'" Unbelief is the primary damning sin.

Fourth, babies are not innocent of the imputed sin of Adam, but they are innocent of personal sin because they have not had the opportunity to personally rebel against God. A number of thought-provoking verses support this assertion.

God said to Jonah, "'And should not I pity Nineveh, that great city, in which there are more than 120,000 persons who do not know their right hand from their left?'" (Jonah 4:11). In his excellent sermon series titled *What Happens to Babies Who Die?* Dr. John MacArthur asserts that these people who did not know their right hand from their left must have been children. These 120,000 children were part of the reason God wanted to save Nineveh. God said they deserved His compassion.

When Moses was about to die, he recounted God telling the Israelites who would enter the Promised Land: "'And as for your little ones, who you said would become a prey, and your children, who today have no knowledge of good or evil, they shall go in there. And to them I will give it, and they shall possess it'" (Deut. 1:39). God said that the children of the rebellious Israelites had no knowledge of good and evil.

God commanded Jeremiah to prophesy these words to the kings of Judah and the people of Jerusalem: "'The people have forsaken me and have profaned this place by making offerings in it to other gods whom neither they nor their fathers nor the kings of Judah have known; and . . . they have filled this place with the blood of innocents'" (Jer. 19:4). Idolatrous Israelites had sacrificed their children to other gods, but the children were not culpable—God called them "innocents."

Paul writes, "His invisible attributes, namely, his eternal power and divine nature, have been clearly perceived, ever since the creation of the world, in the things that have been made. So they are without excuse" (Rom. 1:20). This statement is not true of infants. They have not seen and perceived, and because of that, in some ways, they are "*with* excuse."

Fifth, in the New Testament, we find verses that speak

of God's salvation of individuals from all "people groups" that have ever lived. For instance, Revelation 5:9 records a heavenly song of praise to Christ: "'Worthy are you to take the scroll and to open its seals, for you were slain, and by your blood you ransomed people for God from every tribe and language and people and nation.'"

If we assume there have been people groups that have died without ever hearing about Christ, how can every "tribe" be represented in heaven? This is possible only if children from those tribes died and were saved by the special grace of God. This understanding makes this verse much easier to comprehend and allows for a much more practical view of the end times.

Up to this point, we have been discussing the deaths of infants. But when does a child become an adult and take on responsibility for his own eternal destination? What about unborn children who die—including those who are aborted—and mentally retarded or impaired individuals?

MacArthur addresses the point at which people cease to be children in God's eyes. He says it occurs when a person reaches "sufficient mature understanding to comprehend convincingly the issues of law, grace, sin, and salvation."[4]

This condition is not achieved at a specific age. Every child develops at a different rate and reaches the "mature understanding" at a different time in his or her life. Some may mature to this level at 8 while others need until 18. Until the young person meets the requirements of biblical understanding, he is considered a "child" by God.

Since this is the case, it is clear that unborn babies, including those who are aborted, cannot possibly be accountable for their actions and are thus saved through the grace of God. A believing woman who had an abortion in her youth can rest assured that her baby is in the hands of her loving Father in heaven. While she committed the sin of murder, her child was saved by God's grace.

The idea of "mature understanding" also helps us comprehend the fate of mentally retarded or impaired people. These individuals lack the means to express faith. God, therefore, regards them in the same way that He looks at infants and saves them by His grace. This is a great comfort to parents who spend their entire lives caring for mentally handicapped children. The assurance that they will spend eternity in the new heavens and the new earth with their perfected children is a fabulous blessing of God.

It is possible that up to half of the world's population throughout history has died prior to reaching this mature understanding, and millions of babies (unborn and born) continue to die in this world every year. These babies are either populating heaven or hell at an incredible rate. I am convinced that it is heaven that is experiencing the "baby boom."

Therefore, we should not be spending our time here on earth worrying about our children who have died in infancy. They are in heaven with the Lord Jesus. Rather, we should be praying for our children who are old enough to exercise saving faith in Christ and resting in the comfort of knowing that we believe in a loving heavenly Father.

NOTES

1   Charles H. Spurgeon, as quoted in John MacArthur sermon series, *What Happens to Babies Who Die?* (Panorama City, Calif.: Grace to You Ministries, 2001).

2   B. B. Warfield, as quoted in MacArthur, *What Happens to Babies Who Die?*

3   R. C. Sproul, *Now, That's a Good Question!* (Wheaton, Ill.: Tyndale House, 1996), 294.

4   MacArthur, *What Happens to Babies Who Die?*

conclusion

This book has two purposes. First, I want it to be a resource for people who are struggling with the answers to the five "dilemmas" that I have put forward. Second, I want it to be an incentive for thought. In other words, I hope it will be an encouragement to Christians to think through what they believe about these issues and attempt to come to God-honoring conclusions about them.

You may disagree with the conclusions I have come to. I am sure that there are Christians who do. If, however, you find yourself in that camp, please make sure you base your opinions not on what your mind is telling you may or may not be correct, but on what God is telling you in the Scriptures.

If there is one overriding theme to this book, it is the majesty of God. We want to put everything into a nice, neat package that we can understand. But that is not possible. We are not God. We are creatures and He is the Creator. We cannot begin to fathom how great and awesome our

God is. Considering that He can and does do things that our minds believe to be contradictory helps us see how small our capacity for comprehension really is.

The God of this book is the only God I want to believe in. I do not want to have to worry about making the right decisions that will acquire for me the blessing of eternal life. Rather, I want a God who knows everything, has chosen me to live forever with Him, and will allow me to live this life on earth under His providence and blessings.

God is far greater than we understand Him to be. Hopefully, this book has opened your mind to an appreciation for what God has done for you and the great blessings that He has in store for His people. Thank you for reading it.

Now to him who is able to do far more abundantly than all that we ask or think, according to the power at work within us, to him be glory in the church and in Christ Jesus throughout all generations, for ever and ever! Amen. (Eph. 3:20–21)

For Further Reading

Louis Berkhof	*Systematic Theology*
	Manual of Christian Doctrine
Loraine Boettner	*The Reformed Doctrine of Predestination*
James M. Boice	*The Doctrines of Grace: Recovering the Evangelical Gospel* (with Philip Graham Ryken)
	Foundations of the Christian Faith
	Whatever Happened to the Gospel of Grace?
	Recovering the Doctrines that Shook the World
John Calvin	*The Golden Booklet of the True Christian Life*
	Truth for all Time (A Brief Outline of the Christian Faith)
	Institutes of the Christian Religion
Gordon Clark	*What do Presbyterians Believe?*
Leonard J. Coppes	*Are Five Points Enough? The Ten Points of Calvinism*
B. K. Kuiper	*The Church in History*
Steven J. Lawson	*Foundations of Grace*
John MacArthur	*Alone with God*
	Hard to Believe
J. I. Packer	*Knowing God*

The five Dilemmas of Calvinism

Arthur W. Pink	*The Sovereignty of God*
John Piper	*The Justification of God*
R. C. Sproul	*Essential Truths of the Christian Faith*
	Reasons to Believe
	Chosen by God
	What is Reformed Theology?
	Now, That's a Good Question!
David N. Steele	*The Five Points of Calvinism: Defined, Defended, Documented*
	(with Curtis C. Thomas and S. Lance Quinn)
Johannes G. Vos	*The Westminster Larger Catechism: A Commentary*

about the author

Craig Brown graduated from Geneva College, a Reformed Presbyterian school, with a degree in business administration in 1978. He is the president and CEO of Renaissance Nutrition, Inc., a firm that manufactures and markets nutritional products and services to dairy farmers in the Northeastern, Mid-Atlantic, and Midwestern states.

He has served as a ruling elder in both the Orthodox Presbyterian Church and the Presbyterian Church in America.

Craig has been married to his wife, Rebecca, for 31 years and is the proud father of Heather, Christopher, and Victoria.